HEGEL: A GUIDE FOR THE PERPLEXED

DAVID JAMES

continuum

CONTINUUM International Publishing Group
The Tower Building
11 York Road
London SE1 7NX

80 Maiden Lane
Suite 704
New York
NY 10038

British Library Cataloguing-in-Publication Data
A catalogue record for this book is available from the British Library.

ISBN: 0-8264-8536-7 (hardback)
9780826485366
0-8264-8537-5 (paperback)
9780826485373

Library of Congress Cataloging-in-Publication Data
James, David, 1966–
Hegel: a guide for the perplexed / David James.
p.   cm.
ISBN-13: 978-0-8264-8536-6
ISBN-10: 0-8264-8536-7
ISBN-13: 978-0-8264-8537-3
ISBN-10: 0-8264-8537-5
1. Hegel, Georg Wilhelm Friedrich, 1770–1831.   I. Title.
B2948.J36   2007
193–dc22
2006023804

Typeset by Servis Filmsetting Ltd, Manchester
Printed and bound in Great Britain by
Cromwell Press Ltd, Trowbridge, Wiltshire

WITHDRAWN

CONTENTS

CONTENTS

INTRODUCTION

A distinctive feature of the philosophy of G. W. F. Hegel (1770–1831) is the way in which it forms a system. For Hegel, philosophy, as knowledge of the truth, can in fact only be expounded 'as Science or as *system*'.[1] The science of the Idea or the Absolute, that is, Hegel's own philosophy, is therefore 'essentially a *system*, since what is *concretely* true is so only in its inward self-unfolding and in taking and holding itself together in unity, i.e., as *totality*'.[2] Hegel even claims that the history of philosophy is to be understood as a series of systems, each of which is grounded on a particular principle.[3] This historical process, in the course of which one philosophical system replaces another, culminates in Hegel's own philosophical system, as outlined in his *Encyclopaedia of the Philosophical Sciences*, because it combines all earlier principles within itself, thus overcoming the limited standpoint adopted by previous philosophical systems, each of which is grounded on one principle to the exclusion of others.

Hegel's understanding of his own philosophy as the most comprehensive of all philosophical systems implies that his philosophy forms a totality of interconnected moments, whose truth depends on their being comprehended as moments of this totality. This understanding of philosophy as a system gives rise to a problem for anyone seeking to offer a short introduction to Hegel's thought, since the necessity of focusing on certain aspects of his philosophical system at the expense of others appears to run counter to his conception of philosophy, together with its object, truth as a totality of interconnected moments. In other words, given the systematic nature of Hegel's philosophy, a short introduction to his thought can at best provide only a partial account of his philosophical project. It would therefore help if we could identify a single theme that runs throughout Hegel's philosophical system, which consists of a logic, a philosophy of nature, and a philosophy of spirit; for this theme might provide the key to understanding both the internal dynamic governing the development of this system and the principle which serves to unify its various moments. Fortunately, it is possible to identify such a theme, namely freedom.

There are historical reasons as to why the concept of freedom became central to Hegel's thought. To begin with, in 1789, the French Revolution broke out, an event which Hegel, together with his fellow seminarians at the University of Tübingen, the philosopher F. W. J. Schelling (1775–1854) and the poet Friedrich Hölderlin (1770–1843), clearly welcomed.[4] Hegel also appears to have retained his view of the Revolution as a necessary and thus highly significant historical event later in life. There is, for example, a story relating how, on a trip to Dresden in 1820, a time of deep political reaction in Germany, he unexpectedly ordered a bottle of the finest champagne so as to toast the anniversary of the storming of the Bastille, the event which marked the beginning of the French Revolution.[5]

In the case of French Revolution, Hegel seems to think that there is in fact an especially close relation between historical event and philosophical theory; for, in a letter from 1814, he suggests, with reference to his own 1807 *Phenomenology of Spirit*, that the French Republic was based on an inadequate conception of freedom that originated in the Enlightenment and therefore had to pass out of 'its own destructive actuality' over into another land, the land of 'self-conscious spirit'.[6] Hegel is here referring to the way in which the account of the phase of the Revolution known as the Terror that he gives in the *Phenomenology of Spirit* is followed by an account of the moral world-view as exemplified in the moral philosophy of Immanuel Kant (1724–1804), whose critical philosophy provided the main impetus for the development of German Idealism, which culminated in Hegel's philosophical system. Since, as we shall see, Kant's idea of moral autonomy constitutes for Hegel another highly important stage in human history in so far as it involves the progressive realization of freedom, we must assume that German philosophy is meant to complete the world historical process of which the French Revolution is also an essential stage.

By taking the concept of freedom as my guiding thread, I intend to show that Hegel attempts to complete the process that takes on a new impetus with the events of the French Revolution and is then realized in German philosophy by fully incorporating the idea of moral autonomy into his philosophical system. As we shall see, Hegel thinks that the significance of the concept of freedom should not therefore be limited to the domain of ethics but must instead be extended to include religion and even logic. Moreover, as Hegel's claim that the French Revolution's conception of freedom is inadequate already suggests, his philosophy represents an attempt to offer an adequate theory of freedom which identifies what the latter essentially is.

The approach that I adopt will, however, lead me to concentrate on certain areas of Hegel's thought, such as his social and political philosophy, at the expense of others, most notably his philosophy of nature. My neglect of Hegel's philosophy of nature can nevertheless to some extent be justified on the grounds that, in relation to the issue of freedom, nature is subordinate to spirit for Hegel, who makes a distinction between laws of nature and laws of freedom that derives from modern natural law theory.[7] While the concept of freedom will be seen to provide the key to understanding the internal dynamic governing Hegel's system as a whole, together with many details of the areas of his thought that I do cover, I also hope to show that his theory of subjective spirit, objective spirit, and, to a lesser extent, his theory of absolute spirit can be understood in isolation from his speculative logic, even though Hegel sometimes suggests that the latter underpins the other parts of his philosophical system. In this respect, we can to a certain degree avoid thinking of Hegel's philosophy as forming a system in the strong sense that one part of it cannot be understood in isolation from its other parts.

CHAPTER 1

HEGEL'S PHILOSOPHY OF SUBJECTIVE SPIRIT

1. KANT AND FICHTE ON SELF-CONSCIOUSNESS

In his philosophy of spirit, Hegel employs two key concepts, consciousness and self-consciousness, both of which are of great importance in relation to his account of freedom. They also have an essential role to play in the transition from one form of spirit to another. This is because Hegel's account of freedom and his account of the transition mentioned above both involve the idea of overcoming the opposition between the subject and object of knowledge, an opposition which is typical of consciousness, but is, to some extent, already overcome at the level of self-consciousness. In order to understand Hegel's theory of consciousness and self-consciousness, we first need to look at the conception of self-consciousness that is present in the thought of Kant and J. G. Fichte (1762–1814), together with the distinction that they make between it and consciousness.

In his *Critique of Pure Reason*, Kant seeks to identify the conditions of the possibility of experience in general, amongst which he includes self-consciousness, or the transcendental unity of apperception, as he calls it. When he speaks of experience, Kant means the general experience to which all our particular experiences belong; and he identifies these particular experiences with our various perceptions.[1] Kant defines a perception as an appearance combined with consciousness.[2] He also describes perceptions as a type of representation, namely a representation with consciousness.[3] In other words, a perception is a representation which we are conscious of perceiving. The fact that Kant understands the perceptions that constitute our particular conscious experiences to be representations relates to his claim that the unity of apperception must be considered to be a necessary condition of experience, that is, something that must be presupposed in order to explain the possibility of experience; for this claim is based on the idea that, in order to be conscious of the appearances or representations that make up experience in general, the subject of the latter must be capable of ascribing these representations to itself. In other words, the subject of experience must be in the position to think of these representations as being *its* representations, because otherwise the representations in question would have no meaning for it; and there would not, therefore, be any grounds for identifying them as its representations. However, in addition to the requirement that the subject of experience must be in the position to ascribe representations to itself, Kant introduces another requirement because he is trying to explain the possibility of the general experience to which all our particular experiences belong, and not just our consciousness of particular isolated representations.

This second requirement is that the whole manifold of representations, not just single ones, must be grasped as belonging to one single consciousness. This requirement derives from the fact that the general experience whose possibility Kant is attempting to explain is a single organized experience of which each particular experience forms a distinct moment. The subject of such a general experience must therefore be understood as a self-identical one that remains the same throughout all the different experiences which occur as moments of this general experience. Consequently, the subject in question cannot be thought of as the mere by-product of the unification of the single representations of which it is conscious; it must instead be thought to make the unity of consciousness itself possible by remaining identical throughout all its particular experiences.

The need to introduce such a self-identical subject in order to explain the possibility of a single organized experience also provides the main impetus for Fichte's attempt to explain the essential nature of self-consciousness. Just as Kant argues that both the possibility of identifying various representations as being my representations and the possibility of a single organized experience presuppose the unity of self-consciousness, Fichte claims, in the following passage from his *Science of Knowledge* (*Wissenschaftslehre*), that the unity of self-consciousness must be presupposed if I am to recognize various actions as being my actions:

I cannot take a step, move hand or foot, without an intellectual intuition of my self-consciousness in these acts; only so do I know that *I* do it, only so do I distinguish my action, and myself therein, from the object of action before me. Whosoever ascribes an activity to himself, appeals to this intuition. The source of life is contained therein, and without it there is death.[4]

In other words, self-consciousness is for Fichte, as it is for Kant, a presupposition of any form of empirical consciousness, since it must be thought to accompany each and every representation which the subject, as the ground of a single organized experience, ascribes to itself.

The impossibility of recognizing any representation as my own without presupposing the unity of the subject implies another more fundamental act than that of consciousness, an act which Fichte describes as 'the most primordial act of the subject', since it precedes and conditions all other acts of consciousness.[5] This act, in which the self or 'I' (*das Ich*) makes itself into its own object, is identified by Fichte with the concept of the self:[6] for through thinking itself, the self first comes to exist for itself.

The way in which the self is identical with the act through which it constitutes itself leads Fichte to claim that the self posits itself, by which he means that its existence is immediately given through the act of thinking itself, so that: '*To posit oneself* and *to be* are, as applied to the self, perfectly identical'.[7] In other words, the thought of myself and the fact of my existence are inextricably linked, since the former implies the latter, even though I may, by contrast, exist without thinking of myself. I therefore become certain of the fact that I exist as soon as I make myself into the object of my thought.

The identity of the subject and object of thought which Fichte attempts to explain by means of the idea of an act in which the self posits itself means that the act in question is not directed towards an object which remains external to the subject and must therefore be thought to exist independently of the latter. The subject of the act and its object are instead identical; and in this respect Fichte's idea of the self's positing itself can be seen as an attempt to maintain a firm distinction between self-consciousness, in which subject and object are identical, and the consciousness of objects that are other than the subject which is conscious of them. We shall shortly see that

Hegel views the identity of subject and object, which for Fichte distinguishes self-consciousness from other forms of consciousness, as a necessary stage in the overcoming of the opposition between subject and object to which consciousness gives rise.

Fichte's understanding of self-consciousness as an act of self-positing implies, moreover, that the object of which one is conscious is a product of the subject's own activity; and this in turn suggests a link between self-consciousness and the idea of freedom as self-determination. In other words, self-consciousness involves an awareness on the part of the subject of its own unconditioned activity; and in this respect it must again be thought to differ from forms of consciousness in which the object of consciousness is not identical with the subject that is conscious of it, so that the independence of the object limits the subject's activity.

The idea that there is an essential link between self-consciousness and freedom is, as we shall see, one that Hegel is keen to develop. Kant also suggests a link between self-consciousness and the idea of self-determination when he associates the activity of the thinking subject with an unconditioned form of activity by making a firm distinction between the receptivity of intuition and the spontaneity of the understanding. I shall now say something more about this distinction, since it helps to explain the unifying function that Hegel attributes to the self and the opposition between self-consciousness and consciousness of which he speaks.

For Kant there are two basic forms of intuition, space and time, through which a manifold of sensory representations are given us. These discrete representations (e.g. the representation of x existing at a certain point in space and time) can be brought together to form a single unified representation only through an act of synthesis. This act of synthesis is performed by the understanding, which employs certain pure (i.e. non-empirical) concepts or categories, as Kant calls them. The categories constitute the rules according to which a manifold of discrete representations are to be unified into a single organized whole. For Kant, they are in fact laws, because, unlike rules in general, they provide not only the conditions according to which 'a certain manifold can be posited in uniform fashion', but also the conditions according to which the manifold '*must* be so posited'.[8] In other words, the categories constitute the conditions which make experience in general possible, in the sense that experience in general, as well as any particular experiences occurring within it, must be organized in accordance with them so as to constitute a unified experience, as opposed to a confused manifold of discrete representations that do not appear to stand in a law-governed relation to each other.

While the manifold of representations is given through intuition, which, as purely sensory, may amount to nothing more than the way in which the subject is affected by these representations, thus making the subject's relation to them into a purely receptive one, Kant thinks that the combination of the manifold performed by the categories must be viewed as an act of spontaneity, which as 'an act of the self-activity of the subject . . . cannot be executed save by the subject itself'.[9] This claim turns on the idea that since the categories first make experience possible, they cannot themselves be derived from the latter: they are instead laws that the understanding gives to the manifold of representations given through the pure forms of intuition (i.e. space and time).

The role that Kant thus assigns the categories has important implications with respect to his account of the unity of apperception: for he holds the categories to be in an important sense conditions of self-consciousness itself, even though the subject, through its employment of the categories, brings about the single organized experience to which each of its particular experiences belongs. For in so doing, the subject brings about itself, since it is only by uniting a given manifold of representations within a single consciousness that it becomes possible for the subject to think of itself as remaining identical throughout the series of representations of which it is conscious; whereas in the case of the subject's act of ascribing single representations to itself, it could conceivably have as diverse a self as it has representations of which it is conscious. The fact that the subject must employ the categories in order to unite the given manifold of representations in a single consciousness and to be able to think of itself as that which remains identical throughout its various experiences means that the categories are just as much conditions of self-consciousness as they are conditions of experience in general. Kant therefore claims that the analytic unity of apperception (i.e. the self-identity of the 'I') is possible only under the presupposition of a certain synthetic unity (i.e. the unity achieved by means of the categories).[10]

Although, like Kant, Fichte thinks that self-consciousness is a condition of experience in general, we have seen that he tends to view the self's act of thinking itself as providing the conditions of unity upon which the possibility of consciousness depends, whereas for Kant the categories of the understanding are also required. Hegel appears to follow Fichte rather than Kant when he claims that the 'I' is 'pure being-for-itself, in which everything particular is negated and sublated – consciousness as ultimate, simple, and pure'.[11] For this suggests that the 'I' alone functions as the universal within which all its particular determinations are unified; determinations which may be taken to include the subject's sensations, desires, and inclinations, as well as its representations of external objects. Hegel implies, moreover, that all such particular determinations are not merely contained but also unified within the 'I' when he states that I know everything as being mine in such a way that 'I grasp every object as a member in the system of what I myself am'.[12] The fact that Hegel takes the 'I' to perform the unifying function that Kant assigns the categories is also suggested by his description of the 'I' as 'the simple *category*'.[13]

Hegel's adoption of the model of self-consciousness found in the works of Kant and Fichte is evident from the following definition of subjectivity that he gives: '*pure form*, the *absolute unity* of the self-consciousness with itself, in which the self-consciousness, as "I" = "I", is totally inward and *abstractly* dependent upon itself – i.e. the pure *certainty* of itself, as distinct from truth'.[14] For this definition of subjectivity captures some of the essential features of the model of self-consciousness developed by Kant and Fichte. To begin with, subjectivity, as pure form, is here considered in abstraction from any of the determinate features that serve to distinguish one particular 'I' from another particular 'I'. This is a reflection of the way in which Kant and Fichte discuss self-consciousness in terms of its unifying function and, in the case of Fichte, also in terms of the act through which the self posits itself, since this unifying function and act of self-positing must be understood as common to each and every self-consciousness. Second, the term 'I' = 'I' captures the way in which the subject remains self-identical throughout the various experiences that make up the more general experience of which it is the condition. Third, when Hegel speaks of the 'I' as being certain of itself, he can be seen to have in mind the way in which the 'I' posits itself, in the sense that its act of thinking itself necessarily involves the thought of its own existence, so that the 'I''s certainty of itself does not appear to depend on anything other than its own activity (i.e. its act of thinking itself). This self-certainty is, however, a one-sided, and thus inadequate, form of knowledge for Hegel because, as we shall see, the 'I', as merely self-identical, lacks the moment of consciousness. We have already touched upon the reason why Hegel thinks that the type of self-certainty that the self-conscious subject has of itself must be supplemented by the moment of consciousness; for while both Kant and Fichte understand self-consciousness as being a condition of all conscious experience, experience for them involves another element in addition to the subject's self-activity, namely intuition.

In Kant's case, this is because sensible intuition is the medium through which objects are given us. Consequently, the act of ascribing various representations to myself and unifying them into a single organized experience by means of the categories requires that such representations are first given in inner sense at least, which is subject to the determinations of time, while other types of representation, such as the representations of objects external to myself, must also be given in outer sense, which is structured according to the three dimensions of space.

Self-consciousness likewise forms only part of a more general experience for Fichte, even though he understands the proposition which expresses it (i.e. I = I or I am I) to form the basic principle of all knowledge. Although Fichte claims that all experience can be deduced from the possibility of self-consciousness,[15] the fact that experience is also made up of intuitions leads him to introduce another principle in addition to the I = I. This second principle expresses that which stands opposed to, and is other than, the 'I': the not-'I'. This means that although self-consciousness is a necessary condition of experience, it is not a sufficient one, since experience also involves representations, the existence of which cannot be explained in terms of the self-identity and self-activity of the 'I'. Consequently, the 'I' appears to be conditioned by that which serves as the source of its representations, namely the not-'I'. The way in which each individual self-consciousness is conditioned by the not-'I', as the ultimate source of the various representations that the subject ascribes to itself and unifies within itself, means that the not-'I' must be constantly presupposed in order to explain the possibility of experience, even though we may define it in purely negative terms, as Fichte does when he describes the not-'I' as an external prime mover having no other attribute than that of being an opposing force.[16]

The fact that the not-'I' forms a condition of experience raises a problem for Fichte; a problem that is due to his understanding of the relation of different types of philosophy to the question of freedom. Fichte opposes critical philosophy, by which he means his own philosophy and Kant's philosophy as he interprets it, to dogmatic philosophy. While the essence of the critical philosophy is that it postulates an absolute 'I' that is wholly unconditioned and incapable of determination by any higher thing, dogmatic philosophy appeals to what it takes to be the higher essence of the thing (*ens*), thus postulating the existence of a thing-in-itself that is independent of the 'I' and thus stands opposed to the latter.[17] According to Fichte, dogmatism thereby takes everything that appears to be in our consciousness, together with acts that we consider to be products of free will and even the very belief that we are free, to be the product of the thing-in-itself. In other words, all our thoughts and actions are held to be determined by something that remains independent of us, rather than their being the products of our own spontaneous activity; so that every consistent dogmatist must be a fatalist and materialist who denies the freedom and independence of the self.[18] Since the idealist, by contrast, asserts the freedom and independence of the self, dogmatism and idealism, that is, critical philosophy, must be viewed as totally incompatible with each other. Yet Fichte's acceptance of the necessity of presupposing the not-'I', which appears to have the character of a thing-in-itself, in order to explain the possibility of experience, suggests that his own philosophy fails to fully overcome the dogmatic standpoint that he criticizes and to realize the idealist project.

We shall see in Chapter 4 that Hegel criticizes Fichte for failing to eliminate the not-'I' and makes his own attempt to complete the idealist project by doing away with the idea of a thing-in-itself. Hegel nevertheless accepts that the relation to something other than itself is an ineluctable feature of experience for any finite self-consciousness. Hegel's account of self-consciousness differs significantly from Kant's and Fichte's accounts of it, however, because he seeks to show that self-consciousness can be seen as the result of a dialectical process, whereas for Kant and Fichte it must simply be presupposed in order to explain the possibility of experience. I now intend to outline the different accounts that Hegel gives of the way in which self-consciousness shows itself to be the result of a dialectical process so as to introduce his philosophical method, which will be discussed more fully in Chapter 4. I shall then turn to Hegel's account of universal self-consciousness, in which he seeks to show how the moment of consciousness can be retained in such a way as to avoid the conclusion that the thoughts and actions of each individual self-consciousness are determined by something completely other than itself.

2. SELF-CONSCIOUSNESS AS THE TRUTH OF CONSCIOUSNESS

Hegel makes two main attempts to demonstrate the necessity of self-consciousness, that is, its status as an essential moment of spirit, which does not, however, simply form a presupposition into which we can gain no further insight. These attempts differ in accordance with the aims and character of the two works in which Hegel deals most extensively with the concepts of consciousness and self-consciousness: the *Phenomenology of Spirit* and his *Encyclopaedia* philosophy of spirit.

In the *Phenomenology of Spirit*, Hegel's aim is to lead the unreflective natural consciousness to the standpoint of 'absolute knowing', which involves a form of knowledge in which, as we shall see in Chapter 4, thought is both subject (i.e. that which thinks) and object (i.e. that which is thought), whereas the object remains independent of the subject at the stage of consciousness. Hegel also aims to lead the natural consciousness to the standpoint of absolute knowing in a way that will allow this unreflective form of consciousness to understand its adoption of the standpoint in question as the result of its own activity. Both these aims stem from Hegel's wish to demonstrate that absolute knowing is compatible with the right of modern individuals to have an insight into what they hold to be true.[19] I shall later discuss in more detail Hegel's reasons for thinking that such a right exists, and I shall also identify a number of other ways in which he attempts to meet the demands to which this right gives rise. The aims mentioned above are realized, Hegel believes, by means of the dialectical movement which animates the *Phenomenology of Spirit*, a movement that is generated by the tensions involved in the natural consciousness' own attempts to gain knowledge of its object.

In the introduction to this work, Hegel describes the essential structure of consciousness as one that leads the natural consciousness both to distinguish itself from the object of which it is conscious and to relate itself to this same object through the act of knowing it. He therefore makes a distinction between the object in its relation to consciousness (being-for-another) and the object as it is taken to exist independently of this relation to consciousness (being-in-itself). In the latter case, Hegel identifies this apparent independence of the object with the idea of truth. His identification of the idea of truth with the object's independence of consciousness invites the question as to whether it is really possible to know the object as it is in itself: for it is conceivable that the relation of consciousness to the object (i.e. the act of knowing the object) results in a knowledge of the object that does not correspond to how the latter is independently of our cognitive relation to it. Hegel rejects such concerns, however, on the grounds that they presuppose certain ideas about knowledge, such as the fact that it is a tool or medium. Moreover, he develops his own account of the relation of consciousness to its object which allows us to think of the relation of consciousness to the object and the object of knowledge itself as being united in a single experience. Hegel argues, in short, that the distinction between being-for-another and being-in-itself can be understood to fall within consciousness itself, so that experience must be thought to involve the unity of being-for-another, or the relation of knowing, and being-in-itself, or the truth of the object.

Hegel attempts to justify the idea that conscious experience involves the moments of being-for-another and being-in-itself by arguing that consciousness itself introduces the moment of being-in-itself or truth in the shape of its conception of the truth of the object to which it relates itself through the act of knowing. In other words, consciousness provides the criterion used to assess the truth (or lack of it) of its object, so that it is not possible to separate the question of the truth of the object from the question of consciousness' relation to this object. In order to illustrate this point, Hegel employs the terms concept and object to describe the distinction between the object in its relation to consciousness and its truth or being-in-itself, a distinction which, as we have just seen, falls within consciousness itself. He then identifies two ways in which the relation of these terms to each other may be viewed:

1. Concept = knowledge understood as the relation of consciousness to its object *v.* object = that which consciousness takes to be the essence or truth of the object itself.

2. Concept = that which consciousness takes to be the essence or truth of the object itself *v*. object = the object taken in its relation to consciousness, as opposed to how it is independently of this relation.

While in 1 we have the moments of being-for-another and being-in-itself designated by the terms concept and object respectively, in 2 the roles performed by these terms are simply reversed. Hegel thinks that this reversal is possible because the being-in-itself of the object (i.e. its truth) cannot be separated from its being-for-another, that is, its relation to the knowing subject, because the truth of the object is here to be understood as the conception of its essential nature which the subject employs in its attempt to know the object. These different, but essentially identical, ways of describing the distinction between concept and object that Hegel thinks is immanent to consciousness give rise to two questions, which, as we might expect, amount to essentially the same thing: Does the concept correspond to the object? Or does the object correspond to its concept?

In the case of the first question, the procedure that needs to be followed in order to answer it will involve comparing what consciousness experiences in knowing the object with what it itself takes to be the truth of the object; an act of comparison that only consciousness itself can perform. Since this procedure amounts to consciousness comparing what it experiences with what it takes to be the truth or essential nature of the object, consciousness must ask itself if its conception of the essence of the object corresponds to its actual experience of the latter, so that we might equally ask whether the object corresponds to its concept, which is the second question mentioned above. Consequently, consciousness finds itself locked into a process in which it seeks to find out whether or not its conception of what constitutes the truth of the object can in fact be maintained in the course of its actual experience of the object. In other words, consciousness always approaches the object with some conception of what the latter essentially is; yet this conception of the essential nature of the object may be refuted in the course of consciousness' own attempts to assert that this conception does in fact constitute the essence of the object of experience.

A failure on the part of consciousness to maintain its conception of the essence or truth of the object in the face of its experience of the object results in the emergence of both a different conception of the essence of the object and a different object, since although consciousness' experience of the object forces it to change its conception of the object's essential nature, this new conception of the essence or truth of the object in turn determines how consciousness understands the latter. While Hegel takes this process to be immanent to consciousness, it nevertheless involves a relation to the phenomenal world, since the latter forms the immediate environment in which the natural consciousness finds itself. It is therefore the sensible world in particular that initially both shapes consciousness' conception of the essential nature of its object and forms the object of consciousness. I shall now give a brief account of Hegel's account of sense-certainty, so as to give some idea of how he attempts to put the method outlined in the introduction to the *Phenomenology of Spirit* into practice.

For sense-certainty, the essence of the object is taken to be the simple fact that it exists as a particular object which can be picked out from among other possible objects of sense-certainty by means of the different points in space and time that it occupies. This is also true of the consciousness which knows the object, so that 'the singular consciousness knows a pure "This", or the single item'.[20] In other words, consciousness understands its own essential nature to be the same as that of its object, that is, a particular sensible item existing independently of other particular sensible items in space and time. Hegel then identifies a basic problem with consciousness' attempt to maintain this conception of the essence of the object in the face of its experience of the object; a problem that eventually forces consciousness to renounce this conception of the essence of the object, thus giving rise to a new object of consciousness.

The problem in question is that although consciousness holds that the essential nature of the object is its particularity, as determined by its location in space and time, sense-certainty's attempts to assert this conception of the essential nature of the object in the face of its actual experience of this object shows that there is more to its knowledge of the object than the fact that the latter exists as a particular item, which is independent of other sensory items existing at various other points in space and time. For in order to refer to its object and thus distinguish it from other objects given in space and time, sense-certainty makes use of such terms as 'this', 'now' and 'here', which Hegel argues are general terms under which a multiplicity of particulars can be subsumed. Since sense-certainty claims that the essential nature of the object is simply that of a particular sensory item existing independently of other such items in space and time, such general terms cannot be said to figure in its conception of the essence of the object, and the latter therefore turns out to be different from what sense-certainty takes it to be. In short, even in the case of intuition, a conceptual content must be presupposed; and although this type of content does not form part of sense-certainty's understanding of the essential nature of the object, sense-certainty cannot help introducing such conceptual content in the course of its various attempts to assert its original conception of the essential nature of the object.

Hegel seeks to demonstrate that this is truly the case by allowing sense-certainty to make a series of unsuccessful attempts to avoid characterizing its object as anything other than a particular item, as it must do if it is to hold on to its conception of the essential nature of the object. Sense-certainty seeks, for example, to maintain its conception of the object by claiming that a particular 'I' focuses its attention upon the object and thereby manages to refer to it as a particular sensory item that stands in isolation from other such items in virtue of the different points that it occupies in space and time. Yet the 'I' is itself a universal, since it remains the same throughout any changes that occur with regard to the object of consciousness. Moreover, the 'I' is a universal in the sense that, as mentioned earlier, Hegel assigns it the same kind of function as Kant assigns a category, that is, the function of unifying a manifold of discrete determinations. The term 'I' is also a general term that applies to each and every single 'I' which employs this term when referring to itself. The strategy that sense-certainty here employs in its attempt to maintain its conception of the essence of the object fails, in short, because it is once again forced to invoke what is universal in order to justify its conception of the essential nature of its object, which does not include the idea of universality.

The way in which consciousness comes to experience the inadequacy of its conception of the essence of the object forces it to alter its conception of the object of its knowledge, while the object itself changes together with this conception of its essential nature because the latter determines the way in which consciousness understands its object. The second stage of consciousness, which emerges out of sense-certainty, therefore has a new object, the thing with properties, whose corresponding form of knowing is perception. The inherently defective nature of this new conception of the essential nature of the object in turn gives rise to another object and form of consciousness, the phenomenon of force and its law whose form of knowing is the understanding. Yet in the same way as the thing with properties shows itself to be the truth of sense-certainty, and force shows itself to be the truth of the thing with properties, self-consciousness shows itself to be the truth of consciousness as such. In other words, self-consciousness becomes both the essence of the object and the object of experience itself. Hegel thinks that he has thus shown that self-consciousness is the result of consciousness, rather than merely pre-supposing it as a condition of experience, even though it has, in fact, turned out to be such a condition, in the sense that at the level of consciousness as such it is impossible to provide a satisfactory account of the true nature of the object of experience. Hegel's accep-tance of the idea found in Kant's and Fichte's theories of subjectiv-ity that self-consciousness forms a condition of consciousness is, moreover, evident from his claim in the *Encyclopaedia* that self-con-sciousness is the 'ground' of consciousness because self-conscious-ness is always present in the consciousness of objects.[21]

In his *Encyclopaedia* philosophy of spirit, Hegel adopts a different approach, for he here describes the unfolding of the concept of spirit, so that we are presented with a series of moments in which the true nature, or essence, of spirit is gradually made more explicit. While this is to some extent also true of the *Phenomenology of Spirit*, Hegel does not consider the dialectical movement found in the *Encyclopaedia* philosophy of spirit to be generated by a series of experiences which consciousness undergoes and through which it becomes progressively more aware of the inadequacy of its concep-tion of the essence of the object of experience, with its recognition of this fact leading it to make the transition to a higher stage of con-sciousness. The dialectical movement that is meant to demonstrate the necessity of the various moments of spirit is, in fact, largely absent in the *Encyclopaedia*, which for Hegel himself constituted only a set of theses that were to be developed and clarified in his lec-tures. I shall now give an overview of Hegel's account of the devel-opment of the concept of spirit from its most basic form up until the stage of consciousness, for doing so will help us to understand certain features of Hegel's account of the universal self-consciousness of spirit, which, as we shall see, involves the idea of intersubjectivity, that is, the relation of one self-consciousness to another self-consciousness.

Hegel entitles the first section of the philosophy of subjective spirit anthropology. In this section, he describes a series of pre-conscious forms of spirit, beginning with its most indeterminate or 'immediate' form: spirit living at one with the universal planetary life of the natural soul, that is, spirit as determined by such features of the physical world as climate, the change of the seasons, and different times of the day. This starting-point reflects the way in which the philosophy of spirit emerges out of the philosophy of nature, so that spirit both presupposes nature and is the truth of the latter, in the sense that spirit constitutes the new object for philosophical reflection to which the philosophy of nature itself gives rise. As we shall see, the development that spirit undergoes can be characterized as one in which it progressively frees itself from nature; and this is why Hegel describes the identity of the concept of spirit and its object, which is the result of the philosophy of spirit, as the return from nature.[22]

The natural soul then particularizes itself into the different regions of the earth and the different nations inhabiting them, with each national spirit being determined by the nature of the region it occupies. Next, the soul further particularizes itself as an individual subject, though the subject in question is not to be understood as one that is conscious of being a subject. The subject in question is instead simply the locus of a set of natural determinations, such as talent and character. It is also the subject of certain natural processes (e.g. physical growth and the processes of ageing, sleeping and waking, etc.); and it relates itself to other such subjects in a purely natural way (e.g. through sexual relations). Finally, in the case of sensation, spirit experiences its particular determinations as, on the one hand, different from itself, since it does not appear to be their source and thus stands in a passive relation to them. On the other hand, spirit experiences these sensations as its own in the sense that *it* is what experiences them. As a totality of sensations, spirit is the feeling soul, which develops a feeling of self through becoming aware that the particular feelings that it experiences are one and all its feelings.

The particular feelings (e.g. sensations, desires, drives, passions, etc.) that the feeling soul experiences all relate to the soul's corporeality. In the case of habit, the soul begins to assume control over its corporeality, together with a certain degree of indifference towards it, through a process of repetition. For instance, through repeated exposure to a cold or hot climate, it is possible for the subject, as the feeling soul, to get used to sensations of heat or coldness, while, through repeated practice, it may gain greater control over its own body and develop certain physical skills. In the latter case, the soul's corporeality becomes the instrument through which the soul expresses itself. The soul thus becomes both identical with its body, in the sense that the latter serves as the means by which the soul expresses itself, and the power over it, in the sense that the soul uses its body as an instrument.

Hegel terms the unity of the soul and its body that is thus achieved the actual soul. In spite of this unity of the soul and its body, the soul can be viewed as distinct from, and thus opposed to, its corporeality: for the soul's unity with its body is not an immediate one, but is instead one that the soul itself brings about by turning its body into the instrument through which it expresses itself. A firm distinction has therefore arisen between the soul and its corporeality, which, as both its own body and the physical world in general, stands opposed to the soul. This distinction between the soul and its corporeality in turn makes possible the transition to a higher stage of spirit, namely consciousness, which, as we already know, involves an opposition between the subject and the object of consciousness.

Consciousness forms the first moment of the next section of the *Encyclopaedia* philosophy of spirit, which is entitled phenomenology of spirit. The *Encyclopaedia* account of consciousness, like the one given in the *Phenomenology of Spirit*, consists of three distinct modes of knowing the object: the sensory consciousness, perception and the understanding. The relation between the *Phenomenology of Spirit* and the *Encyclopaedia* philosophy of subjective spirit is a close one because the *Phenomenology of Spirit* was originally planned to form the first part of the 'science of knowledge', with logic and the sciences of nature and spirit forming the second part. This science of knowledge came to be replaced, however, by the three parts (i.e. logic, philosophy of nature and philosophy of spirit) of the *Encyclopaedia of the Philosophical Sciences*. Hegel then incorporated what he regarded as the essential parts of the *Phenomenology of Spirit* into the *Encyclopaedia* philosophy of subjective spirit.

As regards the transition from the final shape of consciousness, the understanding, to self-consciousness, this shape of consciousness divides the object into appearance and the inner realm of laws governing appearances. This inner realm of laws then becomes the real focus of the understanding, which discovers that the essence of lawfulness as such is the unity of different determinations standing in an inner (i.e. essential) relation to each other. Hegel holds, for example, that the concepts of crime and punishment are not contingently related to each other, but instead imply each other.[23] This unity of different, but essentially related, determinations is analogous to the way in which the subject of consciousness and the object of consciousness form moments of a single self-consciousness. The understanding, by grasping the essence of lawfulness as such, which applies equally to the knowing subject as to the object of knowledge, is thus able to recognize itself in its object. It is this element of recognition that makes possible the transition from the stage of consciousness to the stage of self-consciousness, in which the subject and the object of consciousness are identical.

Although an identity of subject and object is achieved in self-consciousness, the moment of consciousness, even when it is taken to involve the consciousness of something other than oneself, still has an important role to play in Hegel's account of self-consciousness; for the self-conscious subject is confronted with an object which remains external to it, whether this object is understood to be the external world in general or a particular object within it, including the subject's own body. In this respect, Hegel appears to accept Fichte's view that the not-'I' is an ineluctable feature of human experience. Yet he also describes this relation of the 'I' to that which is essentially other than itself as a contradiction within self-consciousness between itself as self-consciousness and itself as consciousness.[24] Moreover, we shall see that Hegel views this contradiction and its resolution as being inextricably linked with the question of freedom, with respect to both its essence and its possibility.

The way in which Hegel understands the contradiction which falls within self-consciousness in terms of the problem of the existence of something other than the 'I', which remains independent of the latter, is reflected in the first stage of self-consciousness, desire, which, like the struggle for recognition and the master–slave relation that follow it, is common to both the *Phenomenology of Spirit* and the *Encyclopaedia* accounts of self-consciousness. Desire is, for Hegel, the most immediate form assumed by self-consciousness in its attempt to overcome the contradiction between its self-certainty, which comes about through the act of thinking itself, and the absolute independence of the object confronting it.

In the case of desire, self-consciousness attempts to overcome the independence of the object by demonstrating the inessentiality of this object, as when it consumes the latter. The relation of desire to its object is therefore an essentially destructive and selfish one. This relation turns out, however, to be one in which self-consciousness remains tied to its object, since the satisfaction of desire, which can only be of a temporary nature, requires an endless succession of objects. In other words, although self-consciousness is able to demonstrate the nothingness of the individual object of its desire, it must continually presuppose the existence of objects capable of satisfying its desire, so that in this respect the independence of the object as such is never fully overcome.

Hegel thinks that the contradiction within self-consciousness, which is due to the opposition between its own self-certainty and the absolute independence of the object of consciousness, can be resolved only at the level of spirit. By spirit is here meant the social subject which Hegel describes in the *Phenomenology of Spirit* as 'the unity of the different independent self-consciousnesses which, in their opposition, enjoy perfect freedom and independence: "I" that is "We" and "We" that is "I" '.[25]

3. THE UNIVERSAL SELF-CONSCIOUSNESS OF SPIRIT

In the *Encyclopaedia*, universal self-consciousness turns out to be the result of the previous moments of self-consciousness, desire, the struggle for recognition, and the master–slave relationship. According to Hegel, the condition of universal self-consciousness is one in which each individual self-consciousness has absolute independence; yet, through the negation of its immediacy, it does not distinguish itself from others, but instead recognizes them as being free like itself, while these others in turn recognize the first self-consciousness as free.[26] Self-consciousness has therefore become identical with the object of its consciousness in the sense that it no longer experiences the latter as something completely other than itself, but instead recognizes itself in this object. We thus have two distinct features of universal self-consciousness that need to be explained: the absolute independence of each individual self-consciousness in relation to others and the act of recognition, which involves recognizing the object of one's consciousness as being of the same general type as oneself.

In order to understand the second aspect of universal self-consciousness, the act of recognition, we need to look more closely at what Hegel means by the negation of immediacy that allows each individual self-consciousness to recognize itself in other individual self-consciousnesses. To begin with, we must turn to some of the developments that take place in the preceding moments of self-consciousness, since these developments are ones that the moment of universal self-consciousness presupposes.

We have already seen that desire involves an essentially destructive and egoistic relation to its object, and this is equally true of the next attempt that self-consciousness makes to overcome the otherness of the object, even though this time the object in question is another 'I'. The contradiction between the 'I's self-certainty and the independence of the object this time manifests itself in a drive on the part of each 'I' to prove its independence in the face of another 'I'. This relation between two individual self-consciousnesses, in which both have the drive to demonstrate their independence and freedom to each other, leads to a life and death struggle for recognition. This raises the question, however, as to why Hegel thinks that such a struggle for recognition is inevitable; and I believe that in order to answer this question, we need to introduce the background against which the struggle for recognition must be thought to take place.

In both the *Phenomenology of Spirit* and the *Encyclopaedia*, this struggle is considered in abstraction from the condition in which Hegel thinks it takes place, since it is treated as a shape of consciousness as such. Yet according to one of the additions to the *Encyclopaedia* account of the struggle for recognition derived from lecture notes made by Hegel's students, Hegel claims that the struggle for recognition in its most extreme form, as described in this work, can occur only in the state of nature, in which people are present as isolated individuals.[27] Hegel thus suggests that the background to the struggle for recognition is a primitive condition, a state of nature, in which unsocial individuals confront each other in a hostile manner. Indeed, Hegel, like Thomas Hobbes, characterizes the state of nature as a violent and lawless condition dominated by 'uncontrolled natural impulses'.[28] This suggests that the individuals involved in the struggle for recognition are still at the stage of desire when they first confront each other. We shall now see, however, that the struggle for recognition forms part of a process which allows them to go beyond this stage.

The fact that Hegel identifies the background to the struggle for recognition with a state of nature, in which individuals behave towards each other as natural beings dominated by their immediate desires and impulses, allows us to identify the negation of immediacy with the negation of that which is purely natural. This would correspond to the way in which Hegel's account of the pre-conscious moments of spirit that precede self-consciousness all involve natural forms of spirit. Since by immediacy Hegel can be taken to mean the natural and merely given features that serve to distinguish individuals from each other in ways that are not a result of their own activity, we may assume that the negation of immediacy, which makes possible one's identity with others, rests on the capacity to conceive of oneself in abstraction from all such natural and merely given features.

In the struggle for recognition, Hegel identifies this negation of immediacy with the willingness to risk one's life and the attempt to take the life of the other self-consciousness; for by risking its own life and attempting to end the life of another 'I', self-consciousness demonstrates its absolute indifference to all that is purely natural with respect to both itself and the other self-consciousness.[29] In other words, through freely risking its own life and attempting to destroy another self-consciousness in the struggle for recognition, self-consciousness becomes aware of its capacity to transcend the totality of natural determinations which we call life; and in so doing, it becomes conscious of its absolute independence of the latter. The indifference to one's own natural existence and that of the other self-consciousness demonstrated in the struggle for recognition can thus be seen as part of a formative experience, in which human beings become aware of their capacity to conceive of themselves in abstraction from all the given features that serve to distinguish them from others in a purely natural way. Hegel describes this capacity as follows:

> . . . taken abstractly as such, 'I' is pure relation to itself, in which abstraction is made from representation and sensation, from every state as well as from every peculiarity of nature, of talent, of experience, and so on. To this extent, 'I' is the existence of the entirely *abstract* universality, the abstractly *free*.[30]

Consequently, we may think of the standpoint of universal self-consciousness as one in which each individual recognizes that others possess this capacity as well as him- or herself. Self-conscious individuals do not therefore confront each other as merely natural beings, whose peculiar physical and psychological features, which are merely given ones, prevent them from recognizing each other as beings of the same general type. They instead confront each other as free agents, in the sense that they are no longer completely determined by the pre-conscious moments of spirit which Hegel describes in the anthropology section of the *Encyclopaedia*.

This explanation of what Hegel means by the negation of immediacy and how it relates to his theory of universal self-consciousness invites the question as to how the idea of one's identity with others, which appears to involve setting aside the differences that make people into individuals, can be thought together with the idea that each individual self-consciousness retains an absolute independence in relation to others. In other words, a tension might be thought to exist between the negation of one's particular individuality, which is implied by the idea of one's identity with others, and the demand to accept and respect the particularity of both oneself and others, to which the idea that each individual possesses an absolute independence in relation to others appears to give rise; and we have seen that the moment of absolute independence is as essential to Hegel's theory of universal self-consciousness as the moment of recognition. This apparent tension in Hegel's account of universal self-consciousness can be removed, however, if we understand Hegel's conception of the latter as in effect a restatement of the position that Fichte adopts at the end of his deduction of right in the *Foundations of Natural Right*. Such an interpretation involves understanding the particular individuality which becomes possible through the individual's absolute independence in relation to others as being essentially different from the immediate particularity which has to be overcome in order for human beings to recognize each other as beings of the same general type.

In the *Foundations of Natural Right*, Fichte attempts to deduce the concept of right as a condition of self-consciousness. What is of most relevance to us, however, concerns a problem that arises in connection with the part of the deduction in which Fichte attempts to state the conditions that would explain the possibility of the claim with which he begins the deduction. The claim in question reads: '*If a rational being is to posit itself as such, then it must ascribe to itself an activity whose ultimate ground lies purely and simply within itself*.[31] It is evident from this claim that Fichte identifies rationality with the idea of a self-determining act in which the source of action lies completely within the being that acts. This accords with his claim that the character of rationality consists in the fact that that which acts and that which is acted upon are one and the same.[32] We have already encountered an example of such self-determination in Fichte's account of the act through which the self posits itself by thinking itself, since the self is here both the subject and the object of the act in question.

The rational being which forms the subject of Fichte's deduction of the concept of right is a finite one that remains tied to the kind of representational consciousness which, in the *Science of Knowledge*, leads Fichte to claim that the not-'I' must be presupposed in order to explain experience. Since intuition is the source of its representations, the finite rational being's positing of itself must take place in relation to an object that is both other than itself and limited (i.e. finite), that is to say, an object that is subject to the conditions of intuition (i.e. space and time). Consequently, Fichte first identifies this object as the external world, though he goes on to argue that the latter fails to provide the kind of representation that is required for the finite rational being to posit itself for reasons that need not concern us here.[33] The finite rational being can, in short, posit itself as a rational being only by achieving a determinate representation of itself as a rational being; a representation which must itself derive from a determinate intuition.

Fichte identifies the representation which allows the finite rational being to posit itself with the idea of a summons. He describes this summons as one that allows us to think of 'the subject's being-determined as *its being-determined to be self-determining*';[34] and his reasons for doing so are as follows: The summons requires the subject to whom it is addressed to exercise its free efficacy, that is, to choose from among a whole range of possible actions or even to choose not to act at all; the summons does not, however, determine the subject to act in any particular way; and it thus allows the subject to be self-determining. Moreover, the subject becomes aware of its capacity to be self-determining by comprehending the summons, since the latter constitutes a determinate representation in which its freedom and rationality are presupposed. For it only makes sense to summon someone to exercise free choice if one believes that the individual in question has the capacity to do so.

From some remarks that he makes concerning the summons, it is evident that Fichte does not think that the latter needs to be expressed in words. He instead appears to identify it with the more general act of limiting one's own activity; for he associates the summons with an act of self-limitation, in which the being that summons limits its own freedom in favour of the formal freedom of the person to whom the summons is addressed.[35] In other words, the summons consists of a freely made decision to limit one's own activity, together with evidence of this decision as it appears in the sensible world; evidence which may be of a verbal kind, as when one states one's intention not to lay claim to certain physical objects, but may equally involve the performance or non-performance of certain acts from which such an intention might reasonably be inferred.

The summons can therefore be understood as an act of self-limitation by means of which the person to whom the summons is addressed is made to understand that a sphere has been left open to him or her within which he or she may exercise the capacity for free choice without interference from others. In Fichte's own words, the being who summons 'has, in *his* choice, in the sphere of his freedom, taken my free choice into consideration, has purposively and intentionally left a sphere open for me'.[36] The decision to limit one's own activity in relation to others itself also involves an act of free choice, since the being which summons others to exercise their efficacy could have decided not to limit its own activity, and 'the moderation of force by means of concepts',[37] which can be taken to mean the formation of the end not to limitlessly pursue one's natural desires, drives and inclinations by means of violence. In other words, we must presuppose that the being that summons another finite rational being to exercise its efficacy is free and rational, as opposed to its being determined by natural impulse alone, in which case it would have the character of a merely natural being subject to purely mechanical laws.

Since the being which summons another finite rational being to exercise its efficacy must also be held to be self-determining, we are faced with the problem as to how it came to posit itself as a rational being; for, according to Fichte, this act of self-positing is possible for a finite rational being only through its receiving the summons to exercise its efficacy. Fichte's solution to this problem is to claim that we must assume that the relation between finite rational beings is a relation of 'reciprocal interaction through intelligence and freedom',[38] with each rational being recognizing other rational beings as free. In other words, Fichte assumes a condition of mutual recognition in which each finite rational being, by limiting its own activity, summons another finite rational being to exercise its efficacy, while itself being summoned to exercise its efficacy by others limiting their activity.

Fichte thus presents us with a condition in which individuals recognize others as being of the same general type as themselves (i.e. as free and rational) and behave accordingly, which involves limiting their own activity; and we must therefore presuppose that the members of this community of finite rational beings are not determined by natural impulse alone. In this respect, Fichte presupposes what Hegel's account of the struggle for recognition is designed to explain: how it was that individuals came to think of themselves as not being identical with, and completely determined by, the set of merely natural features that taken together constitute life. Moreover, Hegel seeks to explain how human beings learnt to limit their own activity in relation to others in his account of the one-sided form of recognition that is the immediate result of the struggle for recognition, namely the master–slave relation. For the slave is forced to limit his own activity in accordance with the demands of his master, and he thus learns to act in conformity with demands that do not necessarily accord with the promptings of his own particular will. Hegel stresses the necessity of such discipline when he calls the subjugation of the slave's selfishness the beginning of true human freedom, with the trembling of the singularity of the will and the habit of obeying being necessary moments in the formation of every human being; so that no one becomes free and rational without having experienced the discipline which breaks the particular individual's self-will.[39]

The idea that recognizing others as being of the same general type as oneself involves limiting one's own activity in relation to them allows us to reconcile the negation of one's particular individuality, which appears to imply an identity with others, with the demand to accept and respect the particularity of both oneself and others, as is required by the idea that each individual possesses an absolute independence in relation to others. For, according to Fichte, the act of self-limitation, which leaves open for others a sphere in which to exercise their efficacy, makes individuality possible. As he himself puts it,

'I posit myself as an individual in opposition to another particular individual, insofar as *I* ascribe *to myself* a sphere for my freedom from which I exclude the other, and ascribe a sphere *to the other* from which I exclude myself'.[40] In other words, it is only through exercising free choice and pursuing their own private ends that individuals come to distinguish themselves from others in a way that goes beyond their simply exhibiting certain natural differences which, in their mere givenness, cannot be regarded as a result of their own activity. The possibility of exercising free choice and effectively pursuing one's own ends ultimately depends, however, on the agreement of each and every rational being to limit its own activity and thus allow others a sphere in which to exercise their efficacy. Whereas in the absence of such agreement based on mutual recognition, each individual could not, with any certainty, ascribe to him- or herself a sphere of activity in which to exercise his or her efficacy for any longer than the time in which he or she is able to secure this sphere by means of physical force or because no one else has yet laid claim to it. The recognition of others as being of the same general type as oneself is therefore a condition of individuality.

If we understand Hegel's conception of universal self-consciousness as in effect a restatement of Fichte's position at the end of his deduction of right, the tension that might be thought to exist between the idea of one's identity with others and the idea that each individual self-consciousness retains an absolute independence in relation to others disappears. For the individuality in question is not to be confused with the natural features that serve to distinguish individuals from each other in an immediate way; it is instead to be identified with the exercise of free choice, which allows individuals to distinguish themselves from others through the different choices that they make, and thus in a way that results from their own activity. The particular individuality that is overcome is therefore to be understood as the individuality of a merely natural being subject to mechanical laws, while the identity with others implied in the act of recognition demands limiting one's own activity in relation to others, thus leaving open a sphere in which they may determine themselves as individuals through the exercise of free choice. It is in this sense that individuals retain an absolute independence in relation to each other in Hegel's theory of universal self-consciousness.

We shall see in the next chapter that Hegel develops some of the implications of his theory of universal self-consciousness in his account of objective spirit, which he first gave in the *Encyclopaedia* and later developed in his philosophy of right. Hegel's account of the universal sense-consciousness of spirit is also of more general significance because it already provides an example of his conception of freedom. It does so because, as we have just seen, universal self-consciousness is for Hegel a condition in which each individual self-consciousness is independent in relation to others, in the sense that it has been allotted a sphere in which to exercise free choice without interference from others; yet, at the same time, each individual self-consciousness, through the negation of its natural immediacy, does not distinguish itself from others, but instead recognizes them as being of the same general type as itself. The way in which the ideas of absolute independence and identity in otherness are unified in the concept of universal self-consciousness finds expression in Hegel's views on freedom, as is evident from the following passage, in which he describes freedom in connection with the concept of the will:

> Only in this freedom is the will completely *with itself* [*bei sich*], because it has reference to nothing but itself, so that every relation of *dependence* on something *other* than itself is thereby eliminated. – It is *true*, or rather it is *truth* itself, because its determination consists in being in its *existence* [*Dasein*] – i.e. as something opposed to itself – what it is in its concept; that is, the pure concept has the intuition of itself as its end and reality.[41]

Although Hegel here speaks of the will, rather than self-consciousness, we can nevertheless relate the type of freedom described above to his theory of universal self-consciousness because this conception of freedom involves an identity in otherness, as is shown by the fact that when Hegel speaks of the will in its existence, he identifies the latter with something opposed to the will itself. He speaks, moreover, of the will's intuition of itself; and this again suggests a relation to an object that in some sense stands opposed to the will, even if the will discovers itself in this object. Since the will discovers itself in this object, its relation to the latter is not a relation of dependence on something other than itself; the will instead attains an intuition of its own concept, that is, what it itself essentially is, in this object. Hegel associates this intuition of itself with the idea of truth because, as we shall see in Chapter 4, truth for him involves the unity of the concept and objectivity.

For the most part, Hegel's theory of universal self-consciousness allows us to replace the word will with the word self-consciousness in the description of freedom given above. There is, however, one important respect in which the universal self-consciousness of spirit appears not to correspond to this conception of freedom; for in the case of the latter the moment of independence and the moment of identity in otherness are identified with the will itself. The independence of what is other than the will is therefore denied, whereas the independence of the other forms an essential moment of the universal self-consciousness of spirit. As we shall see, Hegel's description of the freedom of the will in this respect anticipates his account of freedom as the being with oneself in one's other as found in his *Logic*. First, however, we need to look at Hegel's theory of objective spirit, in which he attempts to incorporate and deepen certain aspects of his theory of universal self-consciousness in relation to the concept of the will.

CHAPTER 2

OBJECTIVE SPIRIT: THE PHILOSOPHY OF RIGHT

1. RIGHT AS OBJECTIFIED WILL

Hegel characterizes subjective spirit as spirit which has yet to make its concept objective.[1] The term objective spirit, by contrast, suggests that spirit makes or has already made its concept objective in this part of the philosophy of spirit. Hegel's understanding of objective spirit as the part of his system in which the concept of spirit is made objective raises the question as to how exactly the concept of spirit is made objective; and it should here be pointed out that it is the concept of the will which is objectified in the set of determinations that make up Hegel's theory of right (*Recht*).

The role that Hegel assigns the concept of the will in his philosophy of right is reflected in the structure of his philosophy of spirit, in which an account of the will is given after his theory of universal self-consciousness and before he introduces the concept of objective spirit. This is consistent with Hegel's understanding of the relation of earlier moments of his system to later and higher ones, for he views the earlier moments as being contained in the later ones, in the sense that the latter make explicit what is already presupposed in the former. Hegel's account of the universal self-consciousness of spirit must therefore be thought to imply the concept of the will, as indeed is suggested by the way in which Hegel's theory of universal self-consciousness can be understood as in effect a restatement of Fichte's position at the end of his deduction of the concept of right, which, as we saw, involves the acts of limiting one's activity and of determining oneself through the exercise of free choice, both of which imply the act of willing.

Since Hegel's *Encyclopaedia* account of the will concerns the concept of the will, he attempts to identify the essential moments of the will as such. In other words, Hegel is concerned with the concept of the will instantiated in each and every individual will, rather than the incidental and contingent features that characterize the will of any particular individual. In this respect, we may think of Hegel's concept of the will as representing his version of the general will of which Jean-Jacques Rousseau speaks.

Hegel praises Rousseau for making the will into the principle of the state,[2] and, as we shall see, this is due to the fact that Hegel, like Rousseau, understands the state to be an expression of the general will. Hegel also praises Rousseau for making a distinction between the general will and the will of all, but then criticizes him for failing to maintain this distinction.[3] For Rousseau, the general will is meant to be something more than the will of all because it pays attention only to the common interest, whereas the will of all is based on private interest and is no more than the sum total of particular wills.[4] The distinction that Rousseau thus makes between the general will and the will of all invites the question, however, as to whether there is really a significant difference between the common interest, which is the concern of the general will, and the will of all, since in the case of the latter a common good or interest might also be thought to arise when individuals find themselves forced to cooperate in order to pursue their private interests in the most effective way possible. Indeed, we shall see that Hegel thinks that such a common good, which has its ultimate basis in private interest, characterizes modern civil society.

According to Hegel, Rousseau cannot adequately explain the difference between the general will and the will of all because he adopts the theory of a social contract, which involves each individual consenting to submit him- or herself to the authority of the general will so as to preserve his or her life and freedom, and thus appears to turn the general will into a sum of particular wills, whose ultimate basis may be viewed as an enlightened form of self-interest. In this way, Rousseau commits the errors of considering the will 'only in the determinate form of the individual will' and of regarding the universal or general will 'not as the will's rationality in and for itself, but only as the *common element* arising out of this individual will'.[5] Rousseau appears, in short, to confound the general will with the will of all, which is no more than the sum total of particular wills and whose basis is private interest.

In connection with Rousseau's distinction between the general will and the will of all, Hegel claims that the general will is the concept of the will.[6] This claim indicates that, as mentioned above, the will which is objectified in Hegel's philosophy of right should be understood as the concept of the will instantiated in each and every individual will, or, to put it another way, the general will contained in each and every individual will. This understanding of the idea of the general will can be seen to represent an attempt to avoid the problem as to how we might distinguish the general will from the will of all since Hegel identifies the general will with what is already essential to each and every individual will; the general will does not, therefore, need to be generated through an amalgamation of individual wills, as is the case when it is associated with the act of giving one's consent in the theory of a social contract. Hegel is thus also able to introduce the idea of a general will that is universally valid, since the concept of the will applies equally to each and every individual will, irrespective of the differences that arise in connection with the actual content of any particular will. We therefore need to turn to Hegel's concept of the will so as to gain a better understanding of the idea that right is the objectification of this general will.

Hegel outlines the concept of the will in the introduction to his *Elements of the Philosophy of Right*, and he claims that it consists of three moments, with the third moment involving the unity of the two previous moments. He describes the first moment of the concept of the will as follows:

> . . . the element of *pure indeterminacy* or of the 'I''s pure reflection into itself, in which every limitation, every content, whether present immediately through nature, through needs, desires, and drives, or given and determined in some other way, is dissolved; this is the limitless infinity of *absolute abstraction* or *universality*, the pure thinking of oneself.[7]

This is clearly a description of the abstract self-certainty and self-identity of the 'I' = 'I', which comes about through the act of thinking oneself, an act in which the thought of oneself and one's existence are inextricably linked. Hegel calls the possibility of abstracting from every given determination, which he associates with the abstract self-certainty of the 'I' = 'I', negative freedom.[8]

We have already encountered an example of this kind of freedom in relation to his theory of universal self-consciousness, which presupposes that each individual self-consciousness is able to think of itself in abstraction from all the natural features that serve to distinguish it from others, thus allowing it to consider itself as being of the same general type as anyone else who has this capacity. We shall later see, moreover, that Hegel associates this conception of freedom with the arbitrary will or freedom of choice (*Willkür*), which also has an important role to play in his theory of universal self-consciousness as the act through which individuals distinguish themselves from others.

The first moment of the will represents an inadequate account of what the will essentially is, however; for the will cannot be an actual will unless it posits something determinate as its content and object. In other words, since the act of willing always involves the willing of something, the will must make a determinate content (e.g. a certain state of affairs) into the object of its willing so as to be a will in the proper sense of the word. Consequently, Hegel calls the second moment of the will 'the absolute moment of the *finitude* or *particularization* of the "I"'.[9] The second moment of the will again relates to Hegel's account of the arbitrary will and lends support to the interpretation of his theory of universal self-consciousness as in effect a restatement of Fichte's position at the end of his deduction of the concept of right; for, as we saw, it is only through the exercise of free choice that the willing subject determines itself as an individual.

Finally, since both the moment of negative freedom and the moment of particularization are essential features of the will, Hegel claims that the latter is to be understood as the unity of these two moments; a unity which he describes as 'the *self-determination* of the "I", in that it posits itself as the negative of itself, that is, as determinate and limited, and at the same time remains with itself [*bei sich*]'.[10] From this description of the third moment of the will, we can see that Hegel identifies the act of willing as such as a form of self-determination. However, as we shall see, he thinks that there is a higher form of freedom in which the act of self-determination involves the willing of a specific kind of object or content.

In relation to the self-determining character of the will, Hegel makes a distinction between the way in which the will of the person gives itself existence and the way in which the moral subject determines itself. The person and the moral subject thus each have their corresponding forms of right, namely abstract right and morality. As we shall see below, Hegel's accounts of the person and the moral subject give rise to a set of demands and problems with which he attempts to deal in his theory of modern ethical life (*Sittlichkeit*), which shows itself to be necessary in the sense that it both realizes abstract right and morality and overcomes their limitations.

The fact that abstract right and morality are treated as moments of right shows how far Hegel extends the meaning of the term 'right'. His understanding of right as objective spirit already reflects the way in which the German term *Recht* has a wider meaning than the English word 'right', which is conventionally used to refer to a claim or demand that one believes can be justifiably made in relation to other individuals or in relation to social and political institutions. *Recht*, like *ius* in Latin and *droit* in French, can, by contrast, refer to law or the objective conditions to which our subjective will must conform. In the case of law, it can, moreover, refer to the whole basis and system of law, rather than to specific legal statutes. Hegel extends the meaning of the term right even further, however, for he describes right as any existence in general which is the existence of the free will.[11] Hence his claim that right should not be understood as referring only to limited juridical laws, but as the existence of all the determinations of freedom.[12] Abstract right, which I now intend to discuss, fits this general description of right, and accordingly forms an essential, though subordinate, moment of Hegel's theory of right.

2. ABSTRACT RIGHT

Hegel associates abstract right with the concept of personality, and he claims that 'It is inherent in *personality* that, as *this* person, I am completely determined in all respects . . . and that I am finite, yet totally pure self-reference, and thus know myself in my finitude as *infinite*, *universal* and *free*'.[13] The way in which personality involves knowing that one is infinite, universal and free shows that self-consciousness, and the negative freedom that Hegel associates with it, are essential features of personality. For self-consciousness is infinite in the sense that subject and object are identical, so that the object is not external to the 'I' in its self-certainty; and it is universal in the sense that the 'I' can be conceived of in abstraction from the various determinations that it unifies. This capacity to think of the

'I' in abstraction from all natural and merely given forms of determination allows one to think of oneself as not being completely determined by natural impulse, and thus able to set oneself ends. In this respect, it is significant that Fichte, whose deduction of the concept of right clearly influenced Hegel's theory of universal self-consciousness, uses the term person to refer to the individual who exclusively makes choices within the sphere allotted to him or her by others.[14]

The fact that persons have the capacity to conceive of themselves in abstraction from all natural and merely given forms of determination means, moreover, that a person possesses the capacity to objectify the various features of his or her natural existence, such as his or her various desires or drives, in the sense of being able to adopt a reflective attitude towards them. This allows the person concerned to identify him- or herself with them or to resist identifying him- or herself with them. Hegel acknowledges a person's capacity to stand above the given content of his or her will and identify him- or herself with one particular object of concern rather than another in the following passage:

> . . . this content is only a possible one for the reflection of the '*I*' into itself; it may or may not be mine; and 'I' is the *possibility* of determining myself to this or to something else, of *choosing* between these determinations which the 'I' must in this respect regard as external.[15]

A person, through the exercise of free choice, may, in short, make one thing rather than another into the content of his or her will.

One example of this exercise of free choice is to be found in the capacity to rank one's impulses, drives and inclinations in order of preference, so that one is able to choose to satisfy one impulse, drive or inclination at the expense of others. Hegel views the concept of happiness, which he describes as a 'sum total of satisfaction', in which the subject's various drives are brought into harmony with each other,[16] as an example of this capacity to adopt a reflective attitude towards one's natural existence. For the harmonious sum total of satisfaction in question demands a process of reflection, whereby the various drives are estimated and compared with one another; so that 'thought already has some power over the natural force of the drives, for it is not content with the instantaneous, but requires a whole of happiness'.[17] Nevertheless, in spite of the subordination of the merely natural will to the general concept of happiness, the content of the will remains largely a matter of indifference, since the particular content given to the concept of happiness ultimately depends on what each person thinks will make him or her happy. In other words, the concept of happiness involves an essentially negative conception of freedom, which fails to specify what the content of the will should be.

Hegel's concept of personality can thus be seen to contain a number of interrelated features. To begin with, the person is taken to possess the capacity to act independently of natural impulse instead of simply following its most immediate desires, drives and inclinations. Since a person is not completely determined by natural impulse, he or she also possesses the capacity to adopt a reflective attitude towards the impulses, desires, drives and inclinations that constitute his or her natural existence; an attitude which in turn allows each person to choose to identify him- or herself with one object of concern rather than another. A person's capacity to act independently of natural impulse means that each person is also capable of distinguishing him- or herself from other persons through the act of free choice. Finally, since persons are not completely determined by natural impulse, they may be held responsible for their actions.

For Hegel, personality therefore signifies the capacity for right, as well as forming the basis of a distinctive form of right, which he terms abstract or formal right.[18] This form of right is abstract because it does not consider the individual's particular interests and welfare, or the grounds that determine how an individual acts.[19] As we shall shortly see, these subjective features instead belong to the moral standpoint, which concerns the individual's inner world, whereas abstract right is concerned with an individual's actions only in so far as they appear in the external world. Abstract right has a purely negative function in relation to these actions because it restricts itself to the demand not to violate the idea of personality and whatever follows from it. In other words, abstract right demands that one should not act in ways that violate another person's right to exercise free choice, as would happen, for example, if one were to use coercion against another person without any proper justification, or deprive him or her of any legitimate expressions of his or her arbitrary will, by means of either force or deception.

According to Hegel, this largely negative conception of right finds expression in Kant's universal law of right. Hegel describes the latter as 'the *limitation* of my freedom or *arbitrary will* in such a way that it may coexist with the arbitrary will of everyone else in accordance with a universal law'.[20] In other words, right functions to impose limits on the extent to which persons may exercise free choice and pursue their own personal ends, so as to guarantee all persons the same right to exercise free choice, albeit within certain limits. Abstract right thus serves to preserve and protect an important aspect of Hegel's theory of universal self-consciousness: the absolute independence that individuals have in relation to each other in virtue of the fact that they mutually limit their own activity and thus grant each other a sphere in which each person can determine him- or herself as an individual through the exercise of free choice.

Abstract right itself consists of three main stages. The first stage is property, in which the second moment of the will, the moment of finitude or particularization, takes the shape of an attempt on the part of the will to give itself existence in external objects by taking possession of them, by using them, and by alienating them (i.e. by freely disposing of them, as when one sells an item of property to another person). In other words, the essential determination of property is that the will becomes objective, and thus an actual will, in its property.[21] Property therefore constitutes the first existence of freedom.

Hegel's account of property rests on a distinction between persons and things of which Kant gives a definitive account. Kant defines the person as a subject whose actions can be imputed to him, whereas nothing can be imputed to a thing because it is the object of a person's free choice which itself lacks freedom.[22] Kant explains what is involved in this distinction between persons and things when he points out that although I can be constrained by others to perform actions that serve as the means to someone else's end, I can never be constrained by others to have an end.[23] In other words, while another person may use some form of physical or psychological coercion to compel me to perform an action, which serves as the means to one or more of his or her own ends, this does not imply that I must choose to identify myself with the end in question. On the contrary, if I cannot identify myself with it, I have the capacity to refuse to act as the means to its realization, even if it involves risking my own life or livelihood. In the case of a thing, by contrast, it makes no sense to claim that it has the ability to identify or renounce the end towards which it serves as the means, since it lacks the capacity to form ends altogether; and it can therefore only be given an end through a person's act of appropriating it and using it for his or her own ends. This distinction between persons and things corresponds to Hegel's view of the person as an essentially self-determining type of being and his claim that things are 'unfree, impersonal, and without rights',[24] so that human beings have an absolute right of appropriation over all things.[25]

The second stage of abstract right is contract, which involves a relation between two property owners, and thus a relation between two wills, as opposed to one between a will and a thing. We here have another example of how objective spirit both presupposes and realizes an important aspect of Hegel's theory of universal self-consciousness; for the act of entering into a contract presupposes that the contracting parties recognize each other as persons and property owners, that is, as beings that possess the capacity to honour contracts and freely dispose of their property.[26] Although a contract involves the relation of two independent wills to each other, and thus leads to the formation of a common will, each party to the contract nevertheless retains his or her independence and may therefore act in a way that violates the contract (e.g. by refusing to honour the commitments stated in it). This leads to the next stage of abstract right, which Hegel entitles wrong (*Unrecht*).

In its most extreme form, wrong takes the shape of crime; and it is the need to cancel the crime and re-establish the existence of right that legitimizes the punishment of crime. At the level of abstract right the actuality of right is therefore demonstrated through the punishment of crime, so that Hegel is led to describe abstract right as coercive right.[27] This shows, moreover, that the actuality of the universal self-consciousness of spirit, which requires recognizing others as free and limiting one's activity in relation to them, so as to allow them the possibility of exercising free choice, depends on the existence of a coercive power which, when a person is unwilling to limit his or her activity in the appropriate way, either compels the person in question to limit his or her activity or punishes him or her for not having done so. In this respect, coercive right must be thought to presuppose laws and social institutions that for Hegel belong to the more concrete sphere of right which he calls ethical life. Abstract right can therefore also be considered to be abstract in the sense that it is taken in abstraction from the larger social whole of which it forms a moment.

From what has been said above, Hegel's account of abstract right may be viewed as an attempt to develop his theory of universal self-consciousness in connection with the concept of the will and his understanding of right as objectified will. This leads Hegel not only to develop the implications of his theory of universal self-consciousness but also to introduce property as the first existence of the will, as well as contract and wrong, which he thinks result from the concept of property. The concept of wrong in turn leads to the moral standpoint because it involves a relation between the universal will (i.e. right in so far as its actuality is demonstrated through the punishment of crime) and the subjective will of the individual person, who is made subject to this universal will. It is only at the level of the moral standpoint, however, that the precise nature and implications of the relation between the universal will and the subjective, will of the individual become fully explicit. In his account of the moral standpoint, Hegel introduces various forms of the subjective will of all involve some form of self-determination; so that while the capacity to act in a self-determining manner is treated more or less as a given fact in the section on abstract right, personality becomes its own object in the section on morality.[28]

3. THE MORAL STANDPOINT

The first form of the subjective will that Hegel describes concerns the moral subject's demand that it should be able to recognize itself in anything that others allege to be an expression of its own will (e.g. its actions and their consequences). Hegel discusses this demand in his account of responsibility, in which he seeks to avoid the one-sidedness of two opposed views concerning the extent to which an agent should be held responsible for the consequences of its actions: the view which states that we should disregard the consequences of our actions and the view which states that we should judge actions by their consequences alone.[29]

While Hegel rejects the view that we should completely disregard the consequences of our actions, he also recognizes that once a distinction is made between the consequences of an action, which belong to the external world, and the intention lying behind the action, which belongs to the moral subject's inner world, an issue arises concerning the extent to which the agent can be held responsible for the consequences of its actions. In other words, an essential difference might be held to exist between what a person has in mind when he or she acts and what actually happens as a result of his or her actions. Hegel's acceptance of the legitimacy of the distinction between the moral agent's intention and what actually occurs as a result of acting on the basis of this intention leads him to speak of *'the right of knowledge'*.[30] For Hegel, this right is linked to both the moral subject's capacity to reflect on its own activity and the demand to recognize itself in anything that others allege to be an expression of its own will, as is evident from the reasons that he gives for rejecting the view that actions may be judged by their consequences alone.

An example of the view that actions may be judged by their consequences alone is found in the tragedy of Oedipus, who had no reason to believe that it was his father whom he had killed or his mother whom he had married. Yet, in spite of his ignorance of these facts, Oedipus was nevertheless held to be guilty of the crimes of parricide and incest respectively, and even considered himself to be guilty of them. While Hegel argues that Oedipus cannot reasonably be accused of the crime of parricide, he also points out that the legal codes of antiquity attached less importance to the subjective element which finds expression in the concept of responsibility than is the case in the modern world, with its more developed conception of selfhood.[31] Hegel thus suggests that the right of knowledge is characteristic of the modern world. He in fact considers it to be an example of what he calls the right of the subjective will, which he describes as the right of the will to *'recognize* something or *be* something only in so far as that thing is *its own*, and in so far as the will is present to itself in it as subjectivity'.[32] The demand to recognize or to be something only in so far as that thing is my own means that it must be possible to recognize the consequences of an action as the expression of one's own subjective will, so that one is able to achieve an intuition of oneself in the sense that the consequences of one's actions can be seen as manifestations of one's freedom in the external world.

The second form of the subjective will that Hegel describes concerns the way in which an action must be assumed to proceed from an end that the agent wants to realize, an end in relation to which the action is only the means. This final end or intention constitutes the main interest which an agent has in performing an action, and it thus helps to explain what leads an agent to identify itself with its actions and their consequences. For if the agent concerned can be held to have had a motive for performing an action whose consequences could have reasonably been foreseen, we may consider these consequences, and not just the intention behind the action, to be the expression of this agent's subjective will. According to Hegel, the moral agent must be assumed to have such a motive or interest for performing an action; and he therefore appears to accept that having an interest in one's actions forms a necessary feature of human agency in general. Consequently, Hegel claims that the 'moment of the *particularity* of the agent' is contained and implemented in the action and that this 'constitutes *subjective freedom* in its more concrete determination', which he then describes as 'the *right* of the *subject* to find its *satisfaction* in the action'.[33] This in turn leads Hegel to speak of 'the right of *subjective freedom*', which he identifies with the right of the subject's particularity to find satisfaction, with the recognition of this right representing an essential difference between antiquity and the modern age.[34]

Since it concerns the satisfaction of the subject's particularity, the right of subjective freedom can be thought to include the right of individuals to experience, through their actions, the satisfaction of their most basic needs (e.g. the need for food, clothing and shelter), as when they work in order to procure the means of satisfying these needs. It can also be identified with the right of individuals to seek the realization of their own ideas concerning welfare and happiness. The right of subjective freedom, which forms an integral aspect of the more general principle of subjective freedom, therefore concerns the subject's particularity, in the shape of 'its needs, inclinations, passions, opinions, fancies, etc.', whose satisfaction goes by the name of welfare or happiness, either in its particular determination (i.e. the welfare or happiness of the individual) or in its universal aspect (i.e. the welfare or happiness of everyone).[35] The right of subjective freedom can also be associated with the way in which each person determines him- or herself as a specific individual through the exercise of free choice while pursuing his or her own conception of happiness. We shall see, moreover, that Hegel appears to think that even the satisfaction of one's basic needs has to some extent become a matter of free choice in the modern world.

We have so far encountered three specific rights which for Hegel all fall under the principle of subjective freedom: 1) The right of the individual to be held responsible only for those actions that he or she intended, together with those consequences which he or she could reasonably have foreseen as occurring as a result of his or her actions (i.e. the right of knowledge). 2) The right of individuals to identify with the objects of their concern through having an incentive or inclination to pursue the ends that they do (i.e. the right of the subjective will). 3) The right of the individuals to expect that their particularity is taken into consideration, which rests on the fact that each person is a being with certain natural and artificial needs, together with certain opinions concerning how these needs can best be satisfied (i.e. the right of subjective freedom).

In addition to these three rights, Hegel claims that the right to recognize nothing that I do not perceive as rational is the highest right of the subject.[36] The right to rational insight is of great importance in the modern world, in which, according to Hegel, whatever is to achieve recognition 'no longer achieves it by force, and only to a small extent through habit and custom, but mainly through insight and reasoned argument'.[37] As we shall see below, the right to rational insight is expressive of the demand to recognize something only in so far as that thing is my own in the sense that it conforms to my own rational nature. We must first, however, turn to Kant's moral philosophy in order to understand why Hegel introduces this demand. Kant's moral philosophy is highly significant in relation to Hegel's philosophy of right because it involves an attempt to explicate the precise nature and implications of the relation between the universal will and the subjective will that arises in abstract right when the actuality of right is demonstrated through the punishment of crime. In this respect, while the previous forms of the subjective will essentially concern the idea of freedom as it relates to the standpoint of the individual agent, the next form of the subjective will also stands in an essential relation to a universal will which transcends the standpoint of the individual agent because it is held to be valid for each and every individual.

According to Hegel, the will, in its infinite autonomy, first gained a firm foundation and point of departure in the philosophy of Kant because the latter emphasizes how duty involves the pure and unconditioned self-determination of the will.[38] Kant's idea of the will's autonomy rests on the relation between ethics and reason that he seeks to establish in his theory of the categorical imperative, which he considers to be the highest principle of morality. For Kant, morality involves the conformity of actions to universal law as such; and he claims that this formal type of lawfulness finds expression in the categorical imperative, which runs: Act only on that maxim through which you can at the same time will that it should become a universal law.[39] In other words, one must attempt to universalize the proposition that expresses the course of action which one intends to pursue by asking how it would be if everyone acted in the same way. If the course of action can be universalized without giving rise to a contradiction, it can be assumed to be consistent with the demands of morality. Conversely, if the maxim upon which the subject intends to act turns out to be self-contradictory, we must assume that it is an immoral one. One example that Kant himself gives of an application of the categorical imperative to a maxim that has the second kind of result concerns the maxim of increasing my property by denying that I have in my possession a deposit which was entrusted to me by a person who has recently died and left no record of it. Kant argues that the immorality of such a maxim is demonstrated by the way in which its universalization would result in people no longer making deposits.[40] This could be interpreted as meaning that the social practice of making deposits depends on people admitting that deposits have been made to them, so that, as the universalization of the maxim in question shows, the foundations of this practice would be undermined if everyone to whom a deposit had been entrusted chose instead to deny this fact.

Since the categorical imperative has the form of lawfulness as such, both it and any moral commands generated from it must be valid for all rational beings subject to such laws. This in turn allows Kant to develop the idea that the law to which one is subject is at the same time a product of one's own rational will because all genuine moral commands must be thought to issue from the rational will of each and every rational being. Moreover, since all moral duties stem from one's own rationality, human beings, in so far as they are not deranged or at the mercy of each and every natural impulse, must be thought to possess the capacity to legislate their own laws, in the sense that the laws that they obey are equally the products of their own wills. The person who subjects his or her maxims to the categorical imperative thus possesses the capacity to enact universal law through his or her approval or rejection of such maxims. This enactment of universal law can therefore be seen as an act of self-legislation, as opposed to obedience to a law which is merely given and in this sense remains external to the rational will, as when the validity of moral commands is taken to rest on religious authority or custom and tradition. Kant thinks, in short, that, in the case of moral laws, the will of a rational being is not only subject to the law but is subject to it in such a way that it makes the law which it obeys.[41]

This idea of self-legislation underlies Kant's conception of moral autonomy, which leads him to argue that we must presuppose that we are free, since in order to be able to legislate the law to which one is at the same time subject, one must be able to act independently of all external (i.e. natural or contingent) factors. Kant terms this capacity to act independently of all external factors freedom of choice (*Willkür*). The latter represents only a negative conception of freedom, however, whereas positive freedom for Kant is the capacity of pure reason to be of itself practical.[42] In other words, positive freedom consists in the capacity to freely adopt maxims in virtue of their conformity to universal law as such, as the categorical imperative demands. Positive freedom therefore involves the idea of a specific kind of content that ought to form the object of the faculty of freedom of choice for each and every moral subject. We have already seen how Hegel associates negative freedom, which Kant calls freedom of choice, with a particular form of right (i.e. abstract right); and we shall later see that he attempts to incorporate Kant's positive conception of freedom (i.e. moral autonomy) into his philosophy of right. Yet in order to understand Hegel's attempt to do this, we must first look more closely at the importance that he attaches to the right to rational insight.

As mentioned above, Kant's account of the categorical imperative represents an attempt to determine what is to be the content of ethics without reference to tradition or religious authority. In Kant's view, this type of authority, if it has not already been shown to accord with the essential nature of the rational will, can be considered to be the ultimate source of moral value only at the price of introducing heteronomy of the will, that is, the determination of the rational will by something that remains external to it. Hegel likewise speaks of an '*objective* will', which he describes as 'the will immersed in its object or condition, whatever the content of the latter may be'; and, as examples of this objective will, he cites not only the will of the slave or superstitious will but also the ethical will.[43] The objective will can be understood as one that is subject to an alien authority because the slave must constantly obey another person's will and is thus forced to renounce his own will, while the superstitious will accepts certain religious dogmas into which it has no real insight as being true. The inclusion of the ethical will among such examples of the objective will as the slave and the superstitious will implies that the ethical consciousness is also subject to an external authority when it accepts the validity of ethical norms without having any insight into the source of their legitimacy. We shall see that the need to go beyond the standpoint of the objective will has an important part to play in Hegel's philosophy of right and his philosophy of religion, since he attempts to go beyond this standpoint by showing how it is possible to gain rational insight into the various determinations of right and the content of faith.

An important feature of Kant's account of moral autonomy that relates to Hegel's theory of right concerns the way in which it helps to explain the precise nature of the relation between the universal will and the subjective will that emerges at the end of the section on abstract right through the punishment of crime; for Kant's conception of moral duty implies that the subjective will stands in a relation of obligation to the universal will, which is held to be valid for each and every moral subject. At the same time, this universal will can be actualized only through the act of self-legislation that each subjective will performs. Hegel's acceptance of Kant's understanding of the relation of the subjective will of the individual to the universal will is evident from his claim that the good is 'absolutely essential, and the subjective will has worth and dignity only in so far as its insight and intention are in conformity with the good', while 'it is only in the subjective will that the good for its part has the means of entering into actuality'.[44] With regard to the second claim, Kant can be seen to hold the same view because determinate moral duties for him arise through the application of the categorical imperative to particular maxims as performed by the moral subject. Hegel argues, however, that there are a number of problems with Kant's theory of moral judgement in so far as the issue as to how the categorical imperative can be employed to generate determinate moral duties is concerned.

Hegel speaks of the '*empty formalism*' of Kantian morality, which he thinks is due to the fact that 'it is impossible to make the transition to the determination of particular duties from the . . . determination of duty as *absence of contradiction*, as *formal correspondence with itself*, which is no different from the specification of *abstract indeterminacy*'.[45] This criticism turns on the idea that although Kant thinks that the categorical imperative gives rise to determinate moral duties through the moral subject's act of examining whether or not its maxims can be universalized without becoming self-contradictory, he in fact fails to provide a satisfactory account of how the categorical imperative can be employed to decide whether or not it would be morally acceptable to act on the basis of a particular maxim. Hegel's criticisms of Kant on this point centre on the claim that the categorical imperative is ultimately reducible to the law of non-contradiction, so that the endeavour to find out whether a particular maxim does or does not conflict with the demands of morality amounts to the question as to whether or not the maxim in question involves a contradiction. Hegel argues, however, that the law of non-contradiction cannot be used to determine the morality or immorality of a given content, since a tautology and its opposite, such as 'property is property' and 'non-property is non-property', can both be seen to accord with the categorical imperative, as long as absence of contradiction is taken to be the decisive factor.[46]

This in turn suggests that Kant presupposes a given content and is therefore guilty of the kind of dogmatism which his critical philosophy is meant to avoid; for in order to derive any duties from the categorical imperative, he is forced to presuppose the moral value of certain concepts or practices. One example of what Hegel here has in mind is to be found in the example mentioned above of the maxim of increasing my property by denying that I have in my possession a deposit which was entrusted to me by a person who has recently died and left no record of it. As we saw, Kant argues that the immorality of such a maxim is shown by the fact that, if universalized, it would undermine the practice of making deposits. Yet this argument might be thought to presuppose the legitimacy of private property, which forms the basis of this social practice.

In his account of conscience in the philosophy of right, Hegel can be seen to offer another criticism of Kant's theory of how the categorical imperative is to be applied, although he does not specifically aim this criticism at Kant. This criticism suggests that Kant's theory of moral judgement invites the problem of ethical subjectivism; and it forms an integral part of Hegel's attempt to show how the internal development of the moral standpoint results in the subordination of the universal will to the subjective will, which clearly represents a subversion of the central aims of Kant's moral theory.

For Hegel, conscience expresses 'the absolute entitlement of subjective self-consciousness to know *in itself* and *from itself* what right and duty are, and to recognize only what it thus knows as the good'.[47] In other words, conscience affirms the right of the subjective will to recognize nothing as good or true that it does not perceive as rational. Hegel makes a distinction, however, between the true conscience, for which there is an objective system of ethical principles, and the formal conscience, which lacks such an objective system. In the case of the formal conscience, since it lacks an objective content, all that is left is the abstract self-certainty of the 'I', which, according to Hegel, is merely 'the certainty of *this* subject'.[48]

Hegel makes this claim because he thinks that an appeal to conscience alone in order to justify one's actions reduces ethics to a matter of personal conviction, as is evident from the following statement: '*Subjective opinion* is at last expressly acknowledged as the criterion of right and duty when it is alleged that the ethical nature of an action is determined by *the conviction which holds something to be right*'.[49] One problem with this apparent reduction of ethical duty to a matter of personal conviction concerns the fact that an ethics of conviction, Hegel claims, reduces the responsibility for crime and evil to a minimum when it admits the possibility of error.[50] An explanation of what he means by this can be given if we turn to Kant's account of how the categorical imperative is to be applied in particular cases and the role that he assigns to conscience in connection with this issue. For even though Kant understands the categorical imperative to be an objectively valid moral principle, he appears to reduce particular moral judgements to a matter of personal conviction, which he himself admits may be a source of error rather than ethical truth, when he describes how this principle is to be applied by the moral subject to a particular maxim.

For Kant, conscience is 'an unavoidable fact', which he describes as both 'practical reason holding the human being's duty before him for his acquittal or condemnation in every case that comes under a law' and the consciousness of 'an *internal court* in man'.[51] In other words, Kant identifies conscience with the way in which each individual must decide for him- or herself which maxims accord with the categorical imperative. It is, moreover, essential that the moral subject should be the one to decide this: for otherwise the individual concerned would be subject to an external authority, and this would be contrary to the idea of moral autonomy. This understanding of conscience provides the background to a claim that Kant makes which is vulnerable to one of Hegel's main criticisms of the idea of basing ethics on conscience alone. The claim in question is that a conscience which errs is an absurdity; a claim that Kant makes on the following grounds:

> For while I can indeed be mistaken at times in my objective judgement as to whether something is a duty or not, I cannot be mistaken in my subjective judgement as to whether I have submitted it to my practical reason (here in its rule as judge) for such a judgement; for if I could be mistaken in that, I would have made no practical judgement at all, and in that case there would be neither truth nor error.[52]

As we have seen, Kant's moral theory involves applying the categorical imperative to particular maxims, so that it is such maxims which must be submitted to the judgement of practical reason. The idea behind the claim made above thus appears to be that while I can be mistaken in judging a maxim to be a duty (the objective judgement), I cannot be mistaken in thinking that I have submitted the maxim in question to the judgement of practical reason, so as to determine whether or not it is a duty (the subjective judgement). In other words, while I can be mistaken with respect to the judgement which results from my application of the categorical imperative to a given maxim, I cannot be mistaken with respect to the judgement as to whether or not I have applied the categorical imperative to this maxim; for having made the first judgement, which is of the kind x is (or is not) a duty, it would make no sense for me to doubt that I have submitted x to the judgement of pure practical reason. Admittedly, I might doubt that I have applied the categorical imperative correctly, and it would then be incumbent on me to apply it again to the maxim upon which I intend to act until I am fully satisfied that I have determined its moral status. Yet this does not constitute a doubt concerning whether or not I have applied the categorical imperative; it instead concerns a doubt regarding the particular judgement that results from my application of this moral principle.

This implies that all that can be reasonably demanded of someone is that he or she acts in accordance with the dictates of his or her own conscience by earnestly seeking to determine whether or not the maxims that he or she submits to the judgement of pure practical reason agree with the demands of morality. Once a definitive judgement on this matter has been reached, Kant concedes that as far as guilt or innocence is concerned nothing more can be required of the moral subject.[53] To demand instead that conscience itself should be subjected to some kind of test, so as to determine whether or not it has judged correctly, would require the decision of another conscience, which passes judgement on the first conscience, thus leading to an infinite regress.

It is evident from Hegel's account of conscience in his philosophy of right that for him this kind of argument threatens to deprive ethics of any substantial basis. For if one person, who does not doubt that he has applied the categorical imperative correctly, is judged by others, who are equally convinced that they have made the right moral judgement, to have performed an action that is not a duty and may, in fact, even be a crime, there appears to be no way of deciding who is right; in both cases the source of justification is the same, namely the verdict of one's own conscience, which rests on the conviction that one has applied the categorical imperative correctly. In other words, to pursue Kant's legal metaphor, there is no external court to pass verdict on the conflicting verdicts of these two 'internal courts', which possess equal authority in relation to each other, since each individual appeals to the judgement validated by his or her own conscience, beyond which there is no higher authority.

From this we can see that even if Kant's theory of moral judgement were able to explain how determinate moral commands might be generated from the categorical imperative or assessed by means of the latter, the generation or assessment of such determinate moral commands would nevertheless depend on an individual's conviction that he or she has applied the categorical imperative correctly; and, as Kant himself admits, this introduces the possibility of error. Moreover, since Kant denies that there can be any authority independent of conscience itself that could serve as the means of deciding whether or not the categorical imperative has been applied correctly, the fact that an individual's conviction concerning duty is tied up with the application of a moral principle appears to make little difference in the end; for in each particular case the individual concerned may sincerely believe that what he or she takes to be a duty accords with this moral principle, even if others should accuse him or her of lacking moral judgement. Kant's moral theory appears to rest, in short, on the internal application of a rule, and thus fails to provide an external criterion that might be used to decide whether or not the rule has been applied correctly in particular cases.

Hegel, by contrast, seeks to supply such an external criterion, though one into which individuals may achieve rational insight, in the shape of his theory of modern ethical life (*Sittlichkeit*). The failure of the moral standpoint to explain how the subjective will is to be brought into harmony with the universal will thus leads him to claim that 'the objective system of these principles and duties and the union of subjective knowledge with this system are present only when the viewpoint of ethics [*Sittlichkeit*] has been reached'.[54] In other words, a central aim of Hegel's theory of modern ethical life is to provide an objective system of ethical principles and duties that nevertheless incorporates the principle of subjective freedom, which finds expression in the moral standpoint, while overcoming the latter's inherent limitations.

Hegel's criticisms of Kant's moral theory should not therefore be viewed as implying a complete rejection of the latter. On the contrary, for Hegel, Kant's moral theory contains a number of important insights into the nature of human freedom. One such insight concerns the way in which Kant is able to formulate a conception of unconditional duty that involves the idea that the arbitrary will, or freedom of choice, must will a specific kind of content in order for the moral subject to be truly free. As we shall see, Hegel wants to incorporate this positive conception of freedom into his theory of the modern state, so as to explain how individuals might understand the ethical norms to which they are subject as the expression of their own subjective wills. Kant's conception of duty and moral autonomy are not, however, the only features of the moral standpoint which Hegel wishes to incorporate within his theory of modern ethical life; for, as we saw, this standpoint also gives expression to a set of demands that Hegel thinks must also be met in the case of modern ethical life. This brings me to Hegel's theory of civil society, which forms one of the essential moments of modern ethical life, along with the family and the state.

4. CIVIL SOCIETY

As we have seen, the moral standpoint gives rise to four specific rights which for Hegel all fall under the principle of subjective freedom: 1) The right of the individual to be held responsible for only those actions that he or she intended, together with the consequences that he or she could have reasonably foreseen as occurring as a result of his or her actions (i.e. the right of knowledge). 2) The right to identify with the objects of one's concern through having an incentive or inclination to pursue the ends that one does (i.e. the right of the subjective will). 3) The right to expect that one's particularity is taken into consideration, so that one's welfare and happiness, together with the welfare and happiness of all, ought to be guaranteed (i.e. the right of subjective freedom). 4) The right to have insight into what one holds to be good or true, which is itself a variant of the right of the subjective will. I shall now explain how Hegel's theory of civil society serves to incorporate these four rights into his theory of modern ethical life.

The right of the individual to be held responsible for only those actions that he or she intended, along with those consequences which he or she could have reasonably foreseen as resulting from his or her actions, is realized in civil society because the latter contains a legal system which fully recognizes this right. This legal system is, moreover, compatible with the principle of personality, which provides the basis of abstract right, because all individuals are held to be equal before the law. Indeed, such equality for Hegel forms a central principle of the modern state, in which 'I am apprehended as a *universal* person, in which [respect] *all* are identical. A *human being counts as such because he is a human being*, not because he is a Jew, Catholic, Protestant, German, Italian, etc.'[55]

The way in which the right to identify with the objects of one's concern through having an incentive or inclination to pursue the ends that one does is realized in civil society closely relates to the way in which the right to expect that one's particularity is taken into consideration, together with the ideas of welfare and happiness, are realized. For Hegel identifies a number of ways in which individuals are allowed to pursue their own personal ends, which, by their very nature, are ones that they have an inclination to pursue. Many of these ends are, moreover, linked with the arbitrary will, the exercise of which allows persons to determine themselves as individuals, since, as purely personal ones, the ends in question cannot be held to be valid for each and every person, so that the decision to pursue them is an essentially arbitrary one.

One way in which the arbitrary will is allowed to express itself in civil society concerns the type of work that an individual does. Hegel claims that in modern ethical life an individual's choice of occupation is *'mediated by the arbitrary will*, and for the subjective consciousness, it has the shape of being the product of its own will'.[56] In other words, individuals are not, in principle, compelled to do a particular job, although in each individual case one's choice will be limited by such factors as natural ability and one's level of education. Hegel also thinks that the question of the class to which each person belongs is ultimately determined by *'subjective opinion* and the *particular arbitrary will*';[57] for in choosing to practise a trade or enter an occupation, a person at the same time chooses to enter a certain class. This is why Hegel claims that the principle of subjective particularity is denied its rights by Plato, who, in his *Republic*, assigns to the rulers of the state the task of choosing the class to which each individual belongs.[58]

Hegel thus suggests that, in the modern world, even the satisfaction of one's basic needs is mediated by the arbitrary will, since it is through his or her labour that a person comes to procure the means for satisfying these needs, while the type of work that he or she performs is to some extent the result of free choice. The individual's basic needs are satisfied within that which Hegel calls the system of needs. The latter is a condition of mutual dependence characterized by a division of labour, so that while one person labours to satisfy one particular need (e.g. the need for clothing), another labours to satisfy a different one (e.g. the need for shelter). Each individual thereby becomes dependent on others for the satisfaction of his or her own needs, while others depend on this same individual for the satisfaction of their needs.

The system of needs is not, however, restricted to the satisfaction of basic needs; it instead grows ever more complex because human beings, unlike animals, are capable of multiplying and refining their needs, along with the means of satisfying them, which themselves become needs that demand to be satisfied.[59] The way in which civil society accommodates this multiplication and refinement of needs is itself evidence of the extent to which it allows free play to the arbitrary will in the shape of opinion and caprice, since these more refined needs are of an essentially contingent nature. Even one's natural needs can be seen to involve the exercise of free choice, since there is a whole range of possible ways of satisfying them, such as different kinds of food and clothing. It is within civil society, in short, that the negative freedom of the arbitrary will finds its place within Hegel's theory of modern ethical life. It does so, moreover, in a way that links the satisfaction of each individual's particularity, in the shape of his or her natural and non-natural needs, to the concept of happiness, since individuals have their own opinions concerning which needs are to be satisfied so as to make them happy. The fact that the satisfaction of one's needs is possible only within the condition of mutual dependence that Hegel terms the system of needs also means that the welfare of the individual is inextricably linked with the welfare of all. In this respect, even if individual agents act out of self-interest they nevertheless unconsciously bring about a condition that benefits others as well as themselves, so that, as Hegel puts it:

> The selfish end in its actualization . . . establishes a system of all-round interdependence, so that the subsistence and welfare of the individual and his rightful existence are interwoven with, and grounded on, the subsistence, welfare, and rights of all, and have actuality and security only in this context.[60]

For Hegel, the general good which thus arises can only be maintained, however, through various forms of state intervention, such as regulation of the market economy which has its basis in the system of needs, so that it functions in everyone's interests, and the maintenance of society's infrastructure. Moreover, the legal system and an authority charged with law enforcement are necessary in order to guarantee persons the right to exercise free choice and pursue happiness, as they understand it, without unjust interference from others. Civil society thus also presupposes the existence of an authority that performs the functions of drawing up laws and regulations as well as deciding on the best ways of implementing them. Civil society presupposes, in short, the legislative and executive institutions which for Hegel belong to a different sphere of ethical life, the political state.[61]

The idea of a common good that has its basis in a condition of mutual dependence and is preserved by means of the legal system and the public authority has an important role to play with respect to the right to rational insight. In order to better understand the way in which civil society realizes this right, albeit imperfectly, we must turn to the different types of ethical attitude that Hegel thinks can characterize the individual's relation to the determinations (i.e. laws and institutions) of modern ethical life which provide the idea of duty with a determinate content.

To begin with, Hegel describes the subject's relation to the laws and 'powers' of the ethical substance as one that is immediate and closer to identity than even a relationship of faith or trust.[62] Although Hegel here describes the individual's relation to the state as an immediate experience of his or her identity with the ethical powers, the identity in question must in fact be considered to be a highly mediated one in the case of modern ethical life. The ethical attitude that is most characteristic of the latter is therefore not a feeling of immediate identity, but is instead one based on a feeling of faith or trust towards the laws and powers of the ethical substance, a feeling that is, moreover, based on good reasons. This type of relation must be thought to differ from an immediate identity with the laws and institutions of the state because faith and trust arise only with the emergence of reflection, which in this case will be seen to involve the search for good reasons as to why one should have faith and trust in the laws and institutions of the modern state. For a relation of faith or trust implies a separation of the subject from the object of its faith or trust, with the subject making a conscious decision to accept the authority or protection of the object of its faith or trust. Hegel describes the political disposition, or patriotism, as 'in general one of *trust* (which may pass over into more or less educated insight), or the consciousness that my substantial and particular interest is preserved in the interest and end of an other (in this case, the state)'.[63] This description again implies the separation of the subject from the object of its faith or trust, together with a more reflective attitude towards the various determinations of ethical life, than is suggested by the idea of an immediate identity with them; and it is especially the consciousness that my particular interests are preserved in the interest and end of the state that for

Hegel allows modern individuals to have trust and faith in the laws and institutions of the state.

This brings me to the third type of ethical attitude that Hegel mentions, which he describes as 'a relationship mediated by *further reflection*', and an 'insight grounded on reasons' that may begin with 'certain particular ends, interests, and considerations'.[64] The fact that Hegel cites particular ends, interests and considerations as examples of the kind of reason that he has in mind when he speaks of a relationship mediated by further reflection suggests that he is thinking of a form of insight grounded on reasons whose ultimate basis is self-interest, such as the fact that I am best able to realize my own ends and interests by accepting my social roles and acting in conformity with society's norms because the laws and institutions from which these roles and norms derive serve to promote and sustain the condition of mutual dependence in which my ends and interests, together with those of other people, can best be realized. In other words, by acting in conformity with society's norms and accepting their place within society, individuals gain the best chance of maximizing their own happiness and welfare, as well as the welfare and happiness of the people with whom they must cooperate in order to effectively pursue their own ends and interests.

This type of reason, which is arguably one that a contented member of civil society would give him- or herself for conforming to society's norms and accepting his or her place within it, involves a form of rational insight because it does not rest on an unthinking acceptance of one's social world. It instead presupposes that people have developed an idea of certain requirements that need to be met in order for their social world to qualify as a good one, such as the idea that the social order should provide individuals with the chance of achieving happiness and well-being, or, at the very least, should not prove counterproductive in relation to these ends.

Given the importance that Hegel attaches to this type of reasoning in the case of modern ethical life, it is not surprising that he accords particular importance to the institutions of civil society that give rise to a feeling of security and well-being by describing them as 'the firm foundation of the state and of the trust and disposition of individuals towards it' and 'the pillars on which public freedom rests, for it is within them that particular freedom is realized and rational'.[65] When Hegel describes these institutions as the firm foundation of the state and the pillars on which public freedom rests, he can be seen to have in mind the idea that even though the subject's particularity is satisfied by means of them, the way in which these institutions help to accommodate subjective freedom within the modern state in turn leads individuals to identify themselves more closely with the latter and to will its existence. Hegel therefore claims that:

> The principle of modern states has enormous strength and depth because it allows the principle of subjectivity to attain fulfilment in the *self-sufficient extreme* of personal particularity, while at the same time *bringing it back to substantial unity* and so preserving this unity in the principle of subjectivity itself.[66]

In short, modern individuals identify themselves with the ethical substance (e.g. the laws and institutions of ethical life) largely because the principle of subjectivity is realized within the modern state, so that the satisfaction of one's particularity has become inextricably linked with the existence of the state. However, as we shall see below, this type of insight, which represents a distinctive feature of modern ethical life, is not a fully adequate one for Hegel because it fails to explain the essential nature of ethical life as such; and the limitations of this form of rational insight lead him to provide an account of a different, and higher, form of insight into the determinations of right that make up his theory of modern ethical life.

5. ETHICAL LIFE

I have suggested that Hegel's account of the moral standpoint implies a wish on his part to incorporate the Kantian principle of autonomy into his theory of modern ethical life. We have, in fact, already witnessed one example of how he attempts to do so with regard to the right of each individual to enter an occupation or trade of his or her own choosing, since this right can be thought to involve an act of self-legislation, in the sense that by choosing to enter a particular occupation or to practise a certain trade, a person at the same time assumes a social role that brings with it a set of duties. Yet even if the exercise of free choice here involves subjecting oneself to norms that are self-imposed, the relation between the will and its content is an inessential one because the person concerned could have chosen to enter a different occupation or to practise a different trade, thereby subjecting him- or herself to a different set of norms. Kant's theory of moral autonomy, by contrast, expresses the idea of a content that each and every individual ought to make his or her own, irrespective of whether or not one is inclined to do so. Kant thus suggests that the unity of the subjective will of the individual, in so far as the latter adopts moral ends, and the universal will, which finds expression in the moral law, is an essential, rather than contingent, one.

For Hegel, the universal will, which ought to form the content of the subjective will, achieves existence, and thus becomes actual, in the laws and institutions of modern ethical life. He also appears to want to incorporate the unity of the subjective will of the individual and the universal will which we find in Kant's account of moral autonomy because he describes ethical life as 'the unity of the universal will and the subjective will'.[67] This raises the question as to how this unity of the subjective will and the universal will is brought about. The fact that Hegel identifies the universal will with the laws and institutions of modern ethical life suggests that it is brought about through individuals acting in conformity with the norms that derive from these laws and institutions in their relation to the will of the individual. In this respect, Hegel is able to remind us of an important sense in which the laws and institutions of the state depend on the same individuals whose duty is to act in conformity with them; for it is only through the activity of these individuals that the laws and institutions of the state can become actual. We can therefore think of the universal will that is embodied in the various determinations of ethical life as being in this sense the product of the subjective will, which thus brings about its unity with the universal will. Hegel refers to this essential feature of ethical life when he points out that the state has 'its mediate existence in the *self-consciousness* of the individual, in the individual's knowledge and activity'.[68]

At the same time, however, individuals have no grounds for thinking of themselves as being anything more than accidents in relation to their social substance; for even if not just anyone could effectively perform the social role which person x performs, since factors such as natural ability, talent and skill here come into play, this does not mean that the person concerned is completely irreplaceable. In other words, the performance of a social role does not require genius, in which case no one else but this specific person would be capable of achieving the same result; and it is therefore easy to think of such social roles as being performed by other individuals. The laws and institutions of ethical life are not, in short, dependent on this or that specific individual for their existence, even though they could not have come into being and could not continue to exist without individuals making them effective.

The idea that individuals produce the ethical substance, which at the same time determines their thoughts and actions, is also found in Hegel's account of ethical life in the *Phenomenology of Spirit*. In this work he claims that although substance (i.e. the laws and institutions of the Greek city-state) stands, as the universal essence and end, over against the individualized reality (i.e. the individual agent), self-consciousness both raises the individualized reality to the level of substance and brings substance down to the level of this individualized reality, and thus unites the latter with the universal essence.[69] In other words, by acting ethically, the self-conscious agent not only raises itself to the level of the universal will, which is made manifest in the laws and institutions of the state, but also actualizes this universal will, in the sense that the end of its activity (i.e. the ethical substance), which would otherwise exist only in thought, is brought into being and made effective through this self-conscious agent's activity. In this respect, the ethical substance orientates the thoughts and actions of its members while equally being the product of its members' conscious activity. We can here again see the influence of Kant's idea of a self-legislating pure practical reason at work, since the universal will to which the subjective will is subject is here understood as being the product of the agent's own activity in so far as the latter acts in accordance with the demands of this universal will.

The account of ethical life given in the *Phenomenology of Spirit* relates specifically to the ethical life of ancient Greece, however, whereas Hegel clearly distinguishes between the modern form of ethical life and its earlier manifestations, as is evident from his account of civil society, which serves to accommodate the principle of subjective freedom. As we have seen, in the case of modern ethical life Hegel's attempt to accommodate the principle of subjective freedom makes the relation between the subjective will and the universal will into a highly mediated one, with the individual's identification with the universal will being explained in terms of the way in which the state serves to protect and maintain the general good which arises through the need to cooperate with others, so as to realize one's own ends and interests.

The fact that such mediation is necessary implies that in modern ethical life individuals may well act in accordance with the laws and institutions of the modern ethical life more from self-interest than from a sense of duty; and, as Hegel recognizes, this implies a weaker kind of unity of the subjective will and the universal will than is the case when individuals consciously will the universal as such, thus making the latter into the direct object of their freedom of choice. The idea of a common good within which particular ends and interests can best be realized does not, in short, require that we think of individuals as making the universal as such into the end of their activity, since the state can be seen as having the status of the means to an end, whose ultimate purpose is private interest.

Hegel recognizes that this raises a problem concerning the nature of the unity of the subjective will and the universal will that is achieved in modern ethical life when he refers to civil society as the external state or state of necessity.[70] He describes civil society as the state of necessity because it represents a condition which individuals accept as being necessary if they are going to satisfy their own personal ends and further their own interests; while a particular example of the way in which civil society can be understood as the external state concerns the public authority. The latter intervenes in the workings of civil society so as to regulate the economy and preserve public order, and it thus asserts the primacy of the common interest over any particular interests that threaten it. Yet even though the public authority thus sets limits to the exercise of free choice, individuals accept that such state intervention is necessary because their own interests are better served by such intervention on the part of the public authority than by its absence.

In his 1802 *Natural Law* essay, Hegel criticizes Fichte especially for adopting this 'external' conception of the state. In this essay, Hegel speaks of an opposition between real consciousness, that is, the subject and its individual freedom, and that which he variously describes as pure self-consciousness, pure unity, the empty law of ethics and the universal freedom of all;[71] an opposition which might equally be expressed in terms of an opposition between the subjective will and the universal will. Hegel claims that this opposition finds expression in Fichte's theory of right as the presupposition that 'honesty and trust are lost'.[72] This is a reference to a passage in Fichte's *Foundations of National Right* in which he describes 'the law of coercion' as a power which 'is posited as a means for establishing mutual security when honesty and trust do not exist'.[73] According to Fichte, this coercive power is necessary because even if freedom and security could in principle prevail as a result of honesty and trust amongst persons, there is no law according to which honesty and trust can be produced.[74] In other words, the fact that individuals act in an honest manner, and are therefore genuinely deserving of one's trust, is a contingent matter, so that individuals are fully justified in refusing to rely solely on the good will of others.

This lack of assurance regarding the will of another person can in turn only be remedied by the positing of a power which is independent of each and every particular will.[75] Fichte calls this power the common will. Yet in order to preserve itself by means of coercive force, the common will must itself be equipped with a power in relation to which the power of each individual is infinitely small. Fichte calls this power the state power, which includes two elements: the right to judge and the right to execute the judgements it has made.[76] In other words, the law of coercion presupposes the political state in its executive function. If the state authority is to be effective, there must, moreover, be a link between the executive power and the citizens of the state, a link which for Fichte is formed by the police.[77]

Hegel claims that Fichte thus presupposes an absolute opposition between the individual will and the universal will which makes their unification impossible. In other words, Fichte turns the relation between the subjective will and the universal will into an inessential one. This in turn suggests a kind of heteronomy of the will, since individuals cannot view the objective ethical determinations of the universal will as expressions of their own wills, but must instead regard them as external, albeit necessary, limitations on their freedom of choice. Hegel therefore claims that in Fichte's theory of right the oneness of the individual will with the universal will 'cannot be understood and posited as inner absolute majesty', but is instead only 'something to be produced by an external relation, or by coercion'.[78]

Fichte's understanding of the state as merely a protective power also means that the relation of the state to its citizens can be described as an external relation in the sense that the particular is merely subsumed under the universal, as opposed to being genuinely united with the latter. The subsumption of the particular under the universal is exemplified by the legal system, which applies the laws to which all members of civil society are equally subject in particular cases of non-compliance. For the relation of the subjective will to the universal will can here be thought of as a merely contingent one in the sense that an individual might equally have acted in compliance with these laws, in which case his or her subjective will would not have come into relation with the universal will under which it is subsumed. The relation of the universal will to the will of the individual is thus once again an inessential one.

In spite of his criticisms of the state of necessity, which turn on the idea that this conception of the state views the relation of the subjective will to the universal will as a purely external one, Hegel himself clearly accords the state the functions of guaranteeing security and punishing crime. It is therefore not the case that he rejects this conception of the state altogether; the point is rather that it constitutes a limited, and thus inadequate, conception of the state, which is to be replaced by his theory of modern ethical life. Hegel's identification of civil society with the external state or state of necessity implies, moreover, that he thinks there is nothing to prevent us from viewing the contented *bourgeois* as someone who acts in conformity with the norms governing modern ethical life for purely prudential reasons. This point can be further illustrated with reference to the determination of modern ethical life which for Hegel provides the *bourgeois* with his main source of universal activity: the corporation.

The corporation, which is made up of people who pursue the same trade or occupation, forms one of the main institutions of civil society. Membership of a corporation is determined by such factors as the possession of a particular skill or talent; the corporation in fact sets the standards that determine whether an individual is skilled or able enough to practise a trade or occupation. The corporation is thus an important source of official recognition, which provides individuals with a sense of self-identity and self-respect. The corporation also seeks to protect the interests of its individual members, as well as the common interest that binds its members together. In the latter case, representatives are elected to form part of the legislature, thus establishing a link between the corporation and the political state. This means that the relation of the individual members of a corporation to the political state is an indirect one based on the common interest of the corporation; an interest which need not necessarily accord with the universal interest which forms the end of the political state. The corporation thus provides a good example of the limited extent to which modern individuals are for Hegel politically active.[79] This lack of political involvement can by itself be seen to invite an instrumental attitude towards the state, whose main function is held to be that of protecting the lives and securing the property of its members.

Although each individual, as the member of a corporation, becomes part of a wider social group and thus transcends the atomism which otherwise characterizes civil society, the end of the corporation for Hegel nevertheless remains a 'limited and finite' one.[80] This is because, as mentioned above, the direct object of the corporation's activity remains the particular and common interests of its members, which need not correspond to the interests of the universal as such (i.e. ethical life as a whole). In other words, the corporation represents only an enlightened form of self-interest. Consequently, it does not require thinking of the contented *bourgeois* of civil society as someone who consciously makes the universal as such into the end of his activity. Admittedly, individuals may come to pursue in a self-conscious way the common good which is produced as an unintended consequence of the self-interest that otherwise animates civil society.[81] Indeed, the corporation serves as a good example of this pursuit of a common good; for even though a corporation may have come into being through its members realizing that their own interests could be best realized by joining forces and cooperating with others, such qualities as commitment and self-sacrifice will undoubtedly be required if the corporation is to fulfil its original purpose. Yet however significant this change of consciousness may be, the common good that is consciously willed in this way can still be explained in terms of an enlightened form of self-interest. Hegel therefore needs to explain why modern ethical life must be thought to involve a unity of the subjective will and the universal will that is stronger than the external type of relation which arises when the laws and institutions of the state are understood in instrumental terms.

Hegel's attempt to explain how the unity of the subjective will and the universal will can be conceived in terms other than those of an external relation turns, I believe, on his understanding of right as objectified will. We saw in connection with Rousseau's distinction between the will of all and the general will that Hegel understands the latter to be the concept of the will instantiated in each and every individual will, and that right is the objectification of this general will. This in turn means that the set of laws and institutions that make up Hegel's theory of right are identical with the subjective will in the sense that they are simply the objective aspect of the concept of the will. Consequently, individuals need not think of these laws and institutions simply as limitations, albeit necessary ones, on their freedom of choice, which for Hegel represents only one moment of human freedom. Individuals can instead think of these laws and institutions as being the concrete expression of their own wills. When it is understood in this way, this unity of the subjective will and the universal will allows us to understand the various determinations of right as not being alien to the subject. It thus also helps to explain why Hegel can claim that the subject bears witness to these determinations as its own essence and stands in a relationship to them which is immediate and closer to identity than a relationship of faith or trust, even though this identity is a highly mediated one in the case of modern ethical life.

Hegel's understanding of the unity of the subjective will and the universal will that characterizes ethical life suggests one reason why the *bourgeois* of civil society should make the universal as such into the end of his activity, as opposed to willing the laws and institutions of the modern state simply because they represent the best means of realizing his own ends and interests. The reason in question relates to the idea that, in order to be truly free, individuals must will a content in which they are able to gain an intuition of their own freedom, an intuition which, for Hegel, can be gained only in relation to the various determinations of right that make up his theory of ethical life. These determinations taken together as a whole therefore constitute the conditions of the will's becoming for itself what it is in itself, so that in seeking to actualize and sustain the institutions of ethical life through their own activity, individuals come to give their own freedom an objective form, thus allowing them to gain an intuition of their freedom. Hegel therefore speaks of the absolute determination or drive of the free spirit 'to make its freedom into its object – to make it objective both in the sense that it becomes the rational system of the spirit itself, and in the sense that this system becomes immediate actuality'.[82] The rational system in question is the set of interrelated determinations of right that make up Hegel's theory of ethical life, which he therefore describes as 'the realm of actualized freedom, the world of spirit produced from within itself as a second nature'.[83] Hegel here speaks of a second nature because nature is a presupposition that spirit must overcome; and it does so by producing a set of laws and institutions that are commensurate with the idea of freedom in both its negative form (i.e. the arbitrary will or freedom of choice) and its positive form (i.e. autonomy).

This explanation of the unity of the subjective will and the universal will, and of the reason individuals have for making the universal as such (i.e. ethical life as a whole) into the end of their activity, may appear to turn the relation of the subjective will to the universal will into a purely instrumental one, however, since individuals could be seen as consciously willing the universal as such *in order to* realize their own freedom. Yet the content of the subjective will is this time not one possible end among others, as is typically the case with the arbitrary will, but is instead an end that is essential to the subjective will itself, since freedom is, for Hegel, the substance and essential determination of the will, just as weight is the basic determination of bodies.[84] In this respect, an essential difference can be thought to exist between the content of the arbitrary will in so far as it wills what is purely contingent and its content when it wills the totality of conditions (i.e. ethical life as a whole) that are necessary if the concept of the will, which constitutes the essence of each and every individual will, is to become objective.

At the same time, it is clear from Hegel's account of civil society that he thinks many individuals may in fact will the existence of the laws and institutions of modern ethical life on prudential grounds. Hegel does not, therefore, end up equating what individuals would choose if they were rational with what they actually choose, as one of his liberal critics would have it.[85] He instead thinks that modern individuals may well entertain a purely negative conception of freedom, and that this conception of freedom is an integral feature of modern ethical life. On the other hand, Hegel attempts to show that the laws and institutions of the modern state need not be understood merely as limitations, albeit necessary ones, on human freedom, but may also be understood as expressions of the latter.

Hegel's positive conception of freedom raises its own problems, however; for we may ask whether the determinations of right that

Hegel identifies are adequate expressions of the general will which he identifies with the concept of the will instantiated in each individual will. These determinations of right begin with the will's most immediate attempt to objectify itself by taking possession of objects, and they end with the institutions of the political state: the constitutional monarch, who symbolizes the state's sovereignty, the legislature and the executive. Since a later stage of right is for Hegel more concrete and 'more truly universal' than the one that precedes it,[86] we must assume that the final stage of right, the state, is more concrete than all the earlier stages of right because it contains them within itself. In other words, Hegel understands the state to be a politically unified whole which contains all the moments of his theory of modern ethical life within itself, even though he also considers the political state in isolation from the other moments of ethical life, that is, the family and civil society. The state in the broader sense of the term also incorporates the stages of abstract right and morality because it contains institutions, especially those of civil society, whose function is to realize the principle of subjective freedom.

One example of why we might doubt whether Hegel has succeeded in identifying a set of determinations of right that are fully expressive of the concept of the will contained in *each and every* individual will relates to his attempt to accommodate the principle of subjective freedom within his theory of modern ethical life. The example in question concerns the problem of poverty. Hegel views poverty as a consequence of the workings of the market economy which animates civil society, as in the case of the problem of overproduction, when the volume of goods produced lacks a corresponding number of consumers, thus leading to a reduction in the levels of production, which in turn means that workers must be laid off.[87] Hegel also recognizes that poverty is relative because what counts as a condition of poverty within any given society will depend on such factors as how wealthy the society in question is.[88]

Although Hegel considers some possible solutions to the problem of poverty, he appears unable to offer a definitive solution to it.[89] Since the problem of poverty is a consequence of the workings of the market economy, which forms an essential part of his attempt to accommodate the principle of subjective freedom within his theory of modern ethical life, Hegel presents us with the following dilemma:

On the one hand, since it is a necessary consequence of civil society, the problem of poverty cannot be fully solved while civil society is allowed to operate according to its own principle, which is the principle of self-interest. On the other hand, it is not possible to abolish those features of civil society which give rise to the problem of poverty, since these features are necessary in order for civil society to function as the sphere of modern ethical life in which the right of the subject to experience the satisfaction of its particularity by pursuing its own interests finds it realization. This right must, moreover, find its realization in the modern state because the particularity, or finitude, of the will is an essential moment of the concept of the will which becomes objective in the various determinations of Hegel's system of right. Civil society turns out to be, in short, not only the sphere of modern ethical life which accommodates the subject's right to experience the satisfaction of its particularity but also the source of the problem of poverty. It therefore looks as if that which is to satisfy the subject's right to experience the satisfaction of its particularity is itself the cause of some subjects not experiencing the satisfaction of their particularity, so that Hegel's attempt to explain how the moment of the particularity or finitude of the will is objectified in modern ethical life becomes a source of tension within his theory of the latter.

The problem of poverty also appears to be at odds with the right of the individual to have a rational insight into what he or she holds to be good or true. First, because it implies that some individuals will lack good grounds for thinking that their own welfare and interests are inextricably linked with those of the state itself, even though this identity of interest is for Hegel an important form of rational insight in the case of the modern state. Secondly, those individuals who are denied the benefits that civil society has to offer will equally be denied the type of rational insight that comes from thinking of right as the objectification of the concept of the will instantiated in each and every will, including their own subjective wills. Hegel himself appears to acknowledge this problem when, in one of his lectures on the philosophy of right, he concedes that in the case of poverty a sense of 'inner rebellion' takes on the shape of necessity because 'the freedom of the individual has no existence', with the result that the recognition of universal freedom disappears.[90] In other words, although right, as the objectification of the general will, is meant to constitute the existence of human freedom, the fact that some individuals do not experience the satisfaction of their particularity means that they cannot experience their social world as an adequate expression of their own wills. Consequently, freedom cannot be seen as fully realized in the modern state, as long as poverty remains a structural feature of the latter, with this failure to realize universal freedom being due to the very nature of the modern state, which has the market economy as one of its constitutive features. Hegel's recognition of the problem of poverty thus implies that a whole group of individuals within modern society will be justified in claiming that the latter lacks the legitimacy that is claimed to derive from its being the concrete expression of the general will, that is to say, the concept of the will instantiated in each and every individual will.

The problem of poverty can therefore be seen as an example of the way in which Hegel is led to consider the limitations of the modern state, limitations that stem from the discrepancy between what is taken to be the source of its authority in relation to the subjective will and social reality. For Hegel, the limitations to which the state as such is subject become most apparent, however, when we consider the relation of individual states to each other in the course of world history. This brings me to Hegel's philosophy of history, in which he develops certain aspects of his theory of modern ethical life, and which I shall accordingly treat as an extension of his political philosophy in what follows.[91]

6. THE PHILOSOPHY OF HISTORY

In his philosophy of right, Hegel explains the transition to world history in terms of the independence of each sovereign state in relation to other sovereign states. Unlike the relations between persons, the relations between states are not subject to a higher authority which has the power to make and enforce decisions in cases when a dispute arises between sovereign states, as when, for example, one state accuses another of having broken the terms of a treaty. Consequently, recognition between independent states remains a contingent matter, whereas, in the case of the relations between individual persons, it is guaranteed by the laws and institutions of the modern state. When agreement between sovereign states cannot be reached, war may therefore have to decide the issue. While this implies a 'might is right' view of the matter, which appears to have little to do with the condition of right that is the concern of Hegel's theory of ethical life, Hegel nevertheless seeks to establish a link between his theory of right and world history. This link is designed to show that world history, which would otherwise appear to be nothing more than a random series of events, is governed by a rational process.

The link in question relates to the fact that, as we have seen, Hegel understands his system of right to constitute the realm of actualized freedom, in which finite spirit makes its own freedom into its object. This implies that the condition of right is not merely given but must instead arise in the course of a temporal process during which individuals become ever more conscious of their freedom and gradually produce a set of laws and institutions that are fully commensurate with the idea of freedom. World history is, in other words, the record of spirit's efforts to gain knowledge of what it is in itself (i.e. what it essentially is). As we already know, the essence of spirit is for Hegel freedom, which can only become fully actual in a community of rational beings standing in relations of right to each other and in a set of laws and institutions that give these relations an abiding form. In short, Hegel views world history as a necessary, and thus rational, process because it is the progress of the consciousness of freedom.[92]

The need for human freedom to be realized in a set of laws and institutions allows a distinction to be made between the principle of freedom and its application; and it is the application of the principle of freedom which, from the standpoint of a philosophy of history, is the real impetus behind the events of world history. Prior to its application, the principle of freedom must itself have entered human consciousness, however. For Hegel, it does so through the Christian religion, which teaches that the individual as such, as the object and end of God's love, is of infinite value.[93] Hegel connects this teaching not only with the idea that human beings are essentially equal but also with the idea that they are by nature free. In the latter case, his reasons for doing so can be explained in terms of the feature which, according to him, makes human beings more than any other part of creation deserving of God's love, and thus gives them an infinite value.

As we saw from Kant's distinction between persons and things, the former might be understood as essentially self-determining, whereas it makes no sense in the case of a thing to claim that it has the capacity to set itself ends. On the basis of this distinction between persons and things, Kant accords persons an intrinsic value and describes them as ends in themselves, which ought never to be treated merely as means to an end, whereas things are said to possess only a relative value, which allows them to be treated merely as means to an end.[94]

The objection might here be made, however, that the capacity of persons to set themselves ends is not by itself enough to justify their status as ends in themselves, if this is taken to imply that human beings possess a dignity which things lack. After all, the ends which people set themselves can be of such a kind that one might wish that they lacked this capacity altogether. Yet in order to understand why Kant thinks that human beings possess such dignity, we need to bear in mind the distinction that he makes between subjective ends, which may be motivated by self-interest or physical impulse, and objective (i.e. moral) ends, which are valid for all rational beings.[95] It is the capacity of persons to set themselves objective ends or duties, rather than the capacity to set themselves ends in general, which is the true source of their dignity. Kant therefore identifies moral personality with the freedom of a rational being under moral laws, and thus distinguishes it from psychological personality, which is merely the capacity for being conscious of one's identity through the different conditions of one's existence.[96] In short, although the general capacity to set themselves ends is enough to distinguish persons from things, it is only in virtue of the more specific capacity to set themselves objective ends that persons deserve the status of end in themselves.

Hegel, who clearly employs Kant's distinction between persons and things in his account of abstract right, also thinks that the highest form of freedom (i.e. autonomy) consists in the willing of what is universally valid in an ethical sense, though in his case this means the determinations of modern ethical life. In this respect he, like Kant, can be thought to hold the view that the infinite value that persons possess ultimately derives from their capacity to adopt such universally valid ends. Indeed, Hegel himself states that human beings possess the status of ends in themselves in virtue of their participation in the 'end of reason', which involves fulfilling such ends as those of morality, ethics and religiosity.[97]

As we might expect from Hegel's distinction between the principle of universal freedom and its application, the fact that this principle entered human consciousness with the advent of the Christian religion does not mean that it thereby achieved a determinate existence in a set of laws and institutions which is compatible with this principle. The distinction between persons and things in fact provides a good example of this discrepancy between the principle of freedom and the existing social order: for slavery did not cease to exist with the advent of Christianity. The issue of slavery may therefore be used to illustrate the inner dynamic governing Hegel's philosophy of history.

Hegel sees world history as consisting of various epochs, each of which is represented by a particular national spirit that has world historical significance because of the distinctive principle which is embodied in its laws, political institutions, art, religion and even in its philosophy. To begin with, there is the oriental world, in which human beings have yet to free themselves from a purely natural condition. For instance, in caste systems one's position in society is determined by one's birth, rather than through one's own efforts. In this epoch of world history, only one person is free, a patriarchal ruler, who also has the status of a high priest or a god.

Then there is the Greek world, in which the individual lives in harmony with the ethical life that he himself helps to bring about, as in the Athenian democracy, in which all citizens were actively involved in the political process. However, in the Greek world this political freedom comes at the price of only some people being free, since a high degree of political participation on the part of the Greek citizen was made possible by the institution of slavery, which allowed slaves to take care of the everyday needs whose demands would otherwise, as in the modern world, limit the citizen's level of political participation.

The fact that only some are free is equally true of the next epoch in human history, the Roman world. Yet the latter already contains the seeds of the transition to the next and final epoch, the Germanic world, by which Hegel means, broadly speaking, the Christian nations of Western Europe, in which the principle of universal freedom is realized. The transition from the Roman world to the Germanic world is not made possible by the advent of Christianity and its adoption as state religion alone, however; for the Roman world also contains another important development in relation to the actualization of freedom. The development in question concerns the extension of the status of a person, which forms the basis of abstract right, to all citizens of the Roman Empire. At the same time

Roman law, before which all Roman citizens are considered to be equal, reflects the inability of the Roman world to realize the principle which has arisen within it, for it still treats some persons (e.g. slaves) as if they were things.

Hegel seeks to show that Roman law is for this reason essentially incoherent, and reflects a tension within the Roman world itself which ultimately leads to its dissolution, by pointing out that no definition of a human being would be possible within it because the slave could not be subsumed under this definition. Hegel makes this claim in connection with the idea that the more incoherent and internally contradictory the determinations of a system of right are, the less possible it will be to make definitions within it. He states that definitions should contain universal determinations, whereas in Roman law, the status of the slave, which in Kantian terms is that of the means to an end, makes the definition of a human being impossible.[98] For while the slave belongs to the general type 'human being', he cannot be subsumed under the definition given in Roman law of this general type, since, without any proper justification, the definition in question restricts the extension of the concept human being to the Roman citizen. Roman law fails, in short, to recognize the universal which makes a human being a human being, whereas for Hegel:

> . . . if we consider Caius, Titus, Sempronious, together with all the other inhabitants of a city or a country, the fact that they are all men is not something that they simply have in common; on the contrary, it is what is *universal* in them, it is their *kind*, and none of them would be what he is at all without this kind.[99]

In other words, the universal is for Hegel the ground or substance of the individual. In this particular case, the universal is the concept human being, which is logically prior to any of the contingent features which happen to distinguish individual human beings from each other, such as, to use the example of the slave, the fact that he is a barbarian, or was captured in battle and sold into slavery, or was the offspring of someone to whom this happened in the past. There is, in short, no rational basis for according the slave a different status to the one possessed by his master or the Roman citizen in general, since they are all of the same general type. The status of the slave therefore presents itself as a contradictory element within Roman law, and in this respect Hegel can be seen to employ the concept of universality in a Kantian way; for he clearly considers universalizability to be a necessary condition of rational law, a condition which Roman law fails to apply rigorously enough.

We have already seen that in the modern state the idea of equality, together with the principle of subjective freedom, is realized in civil society. It has, in fact, been argued that the historical significance of the French Revolution for Hegel consists in its unlimited extension of the principle of freedom and the implications that this had for the judging of all existing and future constitutions.[100] Such an interpretation accords with Hegel's description of this historical event as one in which 'heaven is transplanted to earth below'.[101] For this description of the significance of the French Revolution could be interpreted as meaning that the principle that human beings as such are free, which first enters human consciousness as a religious teaching, finds its full application in the actual world by means of the French Revolution.

In the *Phenomenology of Spirit* Hegel suggests, however, that the Terror was a necessary consequence of the French Revolution because of the way in which the latter failed to produce a set of determinate laws and institutions of the kind that we find in his theory of modern ethical life. The reason for this failure is that consciousness, which at this stage takes the universal or general will to be the truth, considers any determinate social or political structures to be incommensurate with this universal will; so that 'Universal freedom . . . can produce neither a positive work nor a deed; there is left for it only *negative* action; it is merely the *fury* of destruction'.[102] For example, the government, though claiming to represent the general will, is in fact in the hands of a group of individuals (i.e. a faction), and it thus excludes others from the act of realizing the general will, even though these others, as members of the general will, equally have the right to determine how the latter is interpreted. The universal or general will that Hegel here has in mind relates to the first moment of the concept of the will, which is the will conceived in abstraction from any determinate content; and it is thus a will which, in its abstract self-identity, is the same as any other individual will from which all determinate content has been abstracted.[103] The bearers of such an abstract universal will are therefore all equal in the sense that, in the absence of the second moment of the will, the moment of particularity, there are no grounds for distinguishing between them.

Although the abstract conception of freedom which Hegel associates with the French Revolution needs, in his view, to be supplemented by an account of a determinate set of laws and institutions, this does not mean that the levelling process which the Revolution brought about was not an historically necessary one. Indeed, the kinds of transformation wrought by the French Revolution, such as the abolition of privileges that stem from one's birth, that is to say, the fact of being born the member of a particular social group (e.g. the aristocracy), represent an emancipation from nature that corresponds to Hegel's account of the development of spirit as the overcoming of its presupposition, which is again nature. The introduction of the idea of civil equality corresponds, moreover, to Hegel's rejection of the way in which previous societies, such as the Greek and the Roman world, treated certain individuals as free by birth (e.g. by the mere fact of being born an Athenian or Spartan citizen) or in virtue of one's strength of character or level of culture.[104] Human beings are thus held to be free on the basis of such contingent factors as the circumstances of their birth, which is a merely natural event, and the qualities that they just happen to possess, either because they were born with them or were able to develop them later in life. Hegel, by contrast, holds that human beings are by nature free, in the sense that freedom is part of their concept. In other words, freedom is an essential part of what it means to be a human being.

This conception of what it means to be a human being is reflected in many of the details of Hegel's philosophy of right, as we might expect from a theory of the modern state which holds the latter to be the actualization of human freedom. For example, Hegel argues that the functions and the powers of the state cannot be private property, as would be the case if certain offices could be inherited or sold, practices that were not uncommon in Europe both before and after the French Revolution.[105] The relation between individuals and the functions and powers of the state is instead to be established on the basis of an individual's ability to perform a certain function or fill a certain office. Hegel accordingly states that every citizen must have the possibility of joining the universal estate (i.e. the bureaucracy which forms the executive power of the political state), with proof of ability providing the essential criterion as to whether or not an individual may join it, since individuals are not destined by birth or personal nature to hold a particular office.[106] While this introduces an element of natural inequality, since some individuals will possess the kind of natural ability which allows them to gain more easily the qualifications required for entry into the universal class, Hegel clearly maintains that there should not, in principle, be any bar to individuals joining the latter, as there would be if public offices were the private property of individuals or families, or if, as in the case of feudalism, some individuals (e.g. serfs) were tied to certain occupations.

The importance that Hegel thus attaches to the idea that nature should not be a determining factor in modern ethical life beyond the confines of the family, which is the natural form of ethical life, sits uncomfortably, however, with the way in which he himself appears to make nature into a determining factor within the political state. Since the latter should have the universal interest as such as its end, it surely ought to reflect the emancipation from both nature and private interest, which still have a role to play in the case of the other forms of ethical life, namely the family and civil society. Yet Hegel not only places an hereditary monarch at the pinnacle of the state, but also makes the landed nobility into an essential part of the legislature, and even claims that it is better equipped for its political role than the estates of trade and industry, by which he means, broadly speaking, the urban middle class.[107]

The way in which Hegel here appears to make nature into a determining factor within the political state, contrary to his own understanding of the dynamic governing world history, may be explained in terms of the idea that for him the ideals of the French Revolution needed to be gradually adapted to the historical conditions prevalent in the Germany of his own time.[108] Such pragmatic considerations cannot, however, be used to justify the idea that an hereditary monarch and the landed nobility are necessary objectifications of the general will, whereas it is precisely this understanding of right as objectified will that is meant to furnish the determinations of right with legitimacy. Admittedly, Hegel seeks to demonstrate the necessity of the hereditary monarch and landed nobility so as to provide rational insight into them. Nevertheless, his attempts to do so have, not surprisingly perhaps, been strongly criticized, most notably by the young Karl Marx.[109]

On the other hand, the idea that Hegel's introduction of an hereditary monarch and the landed nobility into his theory of right was motivated by pragmatic considerations might be seen as a reflection of the fact that for him the state exists in the realm of finitude, and can therefore only imperfectly realize the principle of freedom. Another example of this imperfect realization of freedom is, as we saw, the problem of poverty, which Hegel appears to regard as an abiding feature of the modern state. In this respect, it is significant that the concept of freedom has an essential role to play in Hegel's accounts of religion and philosophy, which both belong to the realm of absolute spirit, whereas his accounts of subjective and objective spirit both belong to an earlier stage in his philosophical system, the stage of finite spirit. This brings me to Hegel's theory of absolute spirit, in which, as we shall see, its various spheres undergo a development within time, just as Hegel understands right as forming part of an historical process.

CHAPTER 3

ART AND RELIGION

1. THE RELIGIOUS FUNCTION OF ART

Hegel thinks of art as having once stood in an essential relation to religion, with the weakening of this relation leading these two spheres of absolute spirit to become independent of each other. In the *Phenomenology of Spirit*, Hegel in fact treats what he would later come to call the symbolic and classical forms of art as moments of the section on religion, whereas in the later *Encyclopaedia* he treats art and religion as distinct moments of absolute spirit. This separation of art from religion is then reflected in the separate series of lectures that Hegel gave in Berlin on the philosophies of art and religion. However, although in these lectures Hegel thus appears to treat art and religion as distinct spheres of human thought and activity, he continued to regard both the symbolic and classical forms of art as being inextricably linked with religion. In one of his lectures on the philosophy of art, Hegel even maintains that art is often the only key to a people's religion.[1]

The separation of religion from art for Hegel occurs only with the emergence of the Christian religion. This separation of religion from art is reflected by the way in which the Greek religion of art is followed by an account of the Christian religion in the *Phenomenology of Spirit* and by the way in which, in the *Encyclopaedia*, the section on art is likewise followed by an account of the revealed religion of Christianity. The transition from art to religion in Hegel's philosophical system is therefore not to be understood as a transition from a form of art which is independent of religion to religion; a transition that would make it seem as if art and religion had for Hegel always formed two distinct forms of human thought and activity. The transition in question is instead to be understood as the transition from a form of religion which is essentially related to art to a form of religion which has emancipated itself from art.

In his lectures on the philosophy of art, Hegel claims in fact that art, like religion (i.e. the revealed religion of Christianity), has as its highest vocation the task of bringing the divine to human consciousness.[2] However, as is already implied by the structure of Hegel's theory of absolute spirit, art comes to lose the function of bringing the divine to human consciousness, with this function being taken over by the revealed religion. The reason why art ceases to perform this function relates to a significant difference between the *Phenomenology of Spirit* and *Encyclopaedia* accounts of art and religion; for in the latter Hegel interposes another art form, romantic art, between the classical form of art and the revealed religion. He does so because, as we shall see, the unity of art and religion, which characterizes the religion of art, no longer exists for Hegel in the case of the romantic form of art, so that art becomes independent of religion and religion becomes independent of art.

Hegel treats the symbolic form of art as the first example of the essential link between art and religion that for him characterizes many pre-Christian religions. In the symbolic form of art, a harmonious relation between form and content, the absolute unity of which is for Hegel the mark of the beautiful work of art or the ideal, as he otherwise calls it, has yet to be attained. By content Hegel here means the concept of God, while by form he means the form of intuition in which this content is expressed. The symbolic form of art's failure to exhibit an harmonious unity of form and content is due to the fact that the content, which is the thought of a highest being or essence that is the ground of all finite being, is so indeterminate that it does not lend itself to being portrayed in a particular sensory form. Yet, in spite of this incommensurability of form and content, the symbolic form of art attempts to portray the divine using various natural forms.

Hegel associates the symbolic form of art specifically with certain oriental religions, and, as we have seen, he considers the oriental world to be one that has yet to emerge from a purely natural condition. Yet Hegel also speaks of ancient religions that do not strictly speaking belong to the symbolic form of art because the symbolic as such does not constitute their basic determination. In these religions the divine is instead completely identified with a natural form, as in Zoroastrianism, which Hegel considers to be a kind of pantheism in which the manifold is reduced to a single unified natural phenomenon, namely light.[3] The divine is thus identified with the natural phenomenon of light, whereas the symbolic form of art involves the use of a natural form to express a meaning that is of a spiritual nature, so that the content is not identified with the natural form which serves as its symbol. The non-identity of form and content that we find in the symbolic form of art means that the relation between form and content is one that must be established through human thought and activity. The symbolic form of art is therefore to be seen as a product of spirit, in spite of the fact that it employs purely natural forms in its attempt to express its indeterminate conception of the divine.

While the symbolic form of art strives to express a spiritual content in a sensory form, the indeterminacy of this spiritual content, as mentioned above, prevents it from being portrayed in a particular sensory shape. Since the determinacy of the natural forms in which the symbolic form of art seeks to express its content is essentially incommensurate with this content, the symbolic form of art must remain only a constant striving to express in sensory form its abstract conception of the divine. This is the case even when the symbolic form of art does not employ any one particular natural form, but instead attempts to express its content in the form of natural processes such as those of generation, growth and decay. In its attempt to portray the divine in a sensory form, the symbolic form of art is in fact led to employ natural forms that are ever more boundless and immense, as when, to use one of Hegel's own examples, the Indian god Shiva is first understood simply as that which is negative but is then taken to be a mountain, river and much else besides.[4] In other words, the natural forms that the symbolic form of art employs undergo a constant increase with respect to both their size and number because its indeterminate conception of the divine cannot be adequately portrayed in any particular sensory form.

For Hegel, the incommensurability between content and form that we find in the symbolic form of art is also evidence of a failure on the part of the religious consciousness to know what God is. For the failure of the oriental religions that he associates with the symbolic form of art to express their content (i.e. the concept of God) in sensory form, so as to make this content present to consciousness in a more distinct way, stems from a failure on the part of the religious consciousness to achieve a more adequate understanding of the divine. A clearer understanding of the latter would be achieved, however, if the divine were to be successfully portrayed in a particular sensory form, since the religious consciousness would then enjoy a determinate intuition of its conception of the divine. Yet such an intuition of the divine is precisely what the symbolic form of art cannot achieve on account of the inherent limitations of its abstract conception of the divine.

According to Hegel, an absolute unity of content and form, which would allow the religious consciousness to achieve an intuition of its own conception of the divine, is only possible when that which is to be portrayed (i.e. the content) is by its very nature susceptible to the form of art.[5] The content must, in short, be of such a kind that it easily lends itself to being portrayed in a particular sensory form. For Hegel, the prime example of such a perfect match of content and form is to be found in classical Greek art because the Greeks conceived of the divine in terms of a set of individual gods with human attributes, and were thus able to adequately express this conception of the divine in a particular sensory form, that is to say, in human form.[6] Art therefore fulfils its highest vocation in the world of classical Greece in the sense that it is able to communicate, by means of intuition, the conception of the divine which forms the object of the religious consciousness at this particular stage in human history.

Hegel suggests, in fact, that the Greeks' understanding of the divine was first made possible through art when he cites approvingly the ancient Greek historian Herodotus' claim that Homer and Hesiod gave the Greeks their gods.[7] Hegel appears to have in mind the idea that the artists and poets of Greek society helped to give shape to an inchoate conception of the divine; for Herodotus claims that Hesiod and Homer gave the Greeks their gods by providing the latter with names, offering an account of their descent, and describing their outward forms,[8] rather than their having given the Greeks their gods in the sense of inventing them. Consequently, art was for the Greeks the highest form in which the divine was made present to the religious consciousness; and the Greek religion of art thus allows us to understand what lies behind Hegel's claim that art sometimes provides the only key to a people's religion. The function which art assumed in the Greek world implies, moreover, that it cannot be understood in isolation from the common religious consciousness out of which it emerges, while this religious consciousness itself cannot be understood in isolation from the work of art which helps to bring the divine to consciousness by presenting it in a determinate sensory shape.

According to Hegel, the reciprocal relation that exists between the classical work of art and the common religious consciousness is, however, severely weakened with the advent of Christianity, because an aesthetic mediation of the divine becomes no longer necessary. The reason why this aesthetic mediation of the divine is no longer necessary is that the Christian religion reveals the divine to human consciousness in a form that Hegel considers to be both essentially different from and more adequate than the form of intuition. The form in question is representational thought (*Vorstellung*), which I shall later discuss in more detail. The Christian religion must dispense with the form of sensory intuition because its conception of the divine is one that, like the content of the symbolic form of art, does not lend itself to being presented in a sensible form, even though it is a determinate one, unlike the conception of the divine which the symbolic form of art unsuccessfully attempts to portray in sensory form.

The distinctive content of the revealed religion finds expression in the doctrine of the Trinity, which for Hegel raises the Christian religion above all other historical religions.[9] In order to illustrate why the conception of the divine contained in this doctrine does not lend itself to being expressed in a particular sensory form, but instead requires the medium of representational thought, it might be pointed out that two of the three persons of the Trinity, namely, God the Father and the Holy Spirit, do not, unlike the Greek gods or even the person of Christ, lend themselves to being portrayed as individual persons. For even though in religious paintings God is sometimes portrayed as an individual person, as an old man with a flowing beard, for example, while, in the case of the Holy Spirit, the image of the dove is used, these images are understood to be symbols rather than literal representations of what God and the Holy Spirit are in themselves. It may seem that the historical Christ, like a Greek god, invites a portrayal of him in human form; yet even here a problem arises in relation to Christ's divinity, so that use must once again be made of symbols, such as a nimbus. The Christian conception of God is, in short, simply too intellectual in character to be captured in sensory form; and any attempt to do so will necessarily involve a symbolic mode of representation, in which the mode of presentation proves to be inadequate in relation to the content that is meant to be expressed by means of it.

Consequently, while art, like the revealed religion, is said to have as its highest vocation the task of bringing the divine to human consciousness, these two spheres of absolute spirit differ with respect to the way in which they bring the object that they share in common to consciousness; for while the revealed religion involves a representational form of consciousness, art involves intuition. In short, in the religion of art, the divine is present to consciousness in a way that allows it to be intuited through the senses, whereas the revealed religion represents this same content in doctrines and teachings that are, as we shall see, part thought and part image. This difference of form has important implications for Hegel's understanding of Christian art, since the latter can at best only attempt to portray the same truth that has already been revealed to humanity independently of art in the form of religious doctrine. In this respect, art, in so far as it functions as a vehicle for bringing the divine to human consciousness, has largely become redundant in the Christian world.

The independence that religion thus achieves in relation to art equally results in the independence of art in relation to religion, a fact that Hegel marks by introducing another form of art in addition to the symbolic and classical forms of art, namely romantic art. The way in which art loses its status as the highest form in which the divine is brought to human consciousness does not, however, mean that it has exhausted all the genuine possibilities open to it and is for this reason incapable of any further development, or that it has become an historically uninteresting phenomenon. Hegel has nevertheless been accused of proclaiming the death of art. Indeed, the idea of the 'end of art' is possibly one of the most famous ideas associated with his name. This idea was already being attributed to him by some of the students who attended his Berlin lectures on the philosophy of art. The composer Felix Mendelssohn-Bartholdy (1809–1847), for example, accused Hegel of asserting that German art was 'dead as a doornail'.[10] Yet Hegel's account of the religious function of art does not imply the idea of the death of art, even though he thinks that art is no longer in the position to perform its highest function, which, as we saw, is to bring the divine to consciousness. In the next section,

I intend to further illustrate this point and also to identify another function that art performed in the Greek world with reference to the way in which Hegel contrasts the original (i.e. Homeric) epic with the modern epic, which he associates with a peculiarly modern art form, the novel.

2. THE ETHICAL FUNCTION OF ART

For Hegel the original epic, of which the Homeric epic is the highest expression, marks the point in a people's development at which it goes from the stage of having an indistinct form of consciousness to the stage at which spirit feels itself capable of producing its own world, in which it still knows itself to be at home.[11] Moreover, while Hegel acknowledges that centuries separate Homer from the events which he portrays,[12] so that in this respect the epic poem is later than the life and spirit which it portrays, he thinks that there is, nevertheless, a close connection between the spirit of the poet and the spirit of the world which he brings forth (i.e. the heroic world portrayed in the epic poem) in the case of the original epic.[13] In other words, the mythical world that Homer portrays in some sense corresponds to the world to which the epic poet himself belongs. In relation to the question as to how we are to understand the connection between these two worlds, I now intend to show that what links them together is the fact that the world portrayed in the original epic reveals the essence of the actual world of which, on the one hand, the epic poet is himself a part, and which, on the other hand, he shapes through his art. This will in turn shed light on the idea that the original epic marks the point in a people's development at which it goes from the stage of having an indistinct form of consciousness to the stage at which spirit feels itself capable of producing its own world, in which it still knows itself to be at home.

Hegel's acceptance of the idea that through his art Homer helped to shape the Greek world of which he himself was a member is, as we have seen, evident from the way in which he cites approvingly Herodotus' claim that Homer and Hesiod gave the Greeks their gods. This is not to say, however, that Homer and Hesiod created the gods, for the relation of the Greek artist to the content of his art can be understood as a twofold one. To begin with, this content involves a traditional element, a commonly held understanding of the divine and the past; and Hegel thinks that this traditional element must

belong to a living tradition if there is going to be an essential connection between the world that the epic poet portrays and the world
of which he himself is a member. He is therefore critical of the
attempt made by the eighteenth-century German poet Friedrich
Gottlob Klopstock (1724–1803) to provide Germany with its own
Christian epic, since in this case there is, on the one hand, the story
of the life of Jesus, while, on the other hand, there is German
culture of the eighteenth century, with the result that the understanding of the content belongs to a different age from the content
itself.[14] This separation of the content of the epic from its cultural
conditions for Hegel also distinguishes Virgil, who employs mythology in a purely mechanical way, from Homer.[15] We must therefore
assume that in the case of the original epic the level of culture that
is characteristic of the age in which the poet lives corresponds to the
level of culture found in the world that he portrays. Secondly, there
is an element of innovation, with the artist offering his own interpretation of the traditional elements through his arrangement and
portrayal of them in the work of art. In short, while the world portrayed in the original epic has reference to a pre-existing world,
which is not alien to the world to which the epic poet himself
belongs, the epic poet, through his portrayal of this given content,
helps to clarify this world and give it an abiding form.

In the case of the element of innovation introduced by the epic
poet, his relation to the content of the original epic can be seen to turn
on the idea that it was not only the Greek people's conception of the
divine, but also its conception of the ethical that lacked determinacy,
so that it fell to the Greek artist to give concrete expression to a commonly held, but inchoate, understanding of both the gods and the
ethical norms governing Greek society. In the latter case, though there
may well have been a host of commonly held ideas concerning the
behaviour of the gods and heroes of Greek mythology, the artist's
portrayal of the actions and deeds of these gods and heroes provided
people with an abiding and determinate presentation of them. The
portrayal of the actions and deeds of the gods and heroes, along with
their relations to each other, as given in the original epic, thus helped
to reinforce and perpetuate certain commonly held ideas concerning
what constitutes a noble or base, a devout or sacrilegious, action or
deed; and Hegel himself points to the ethical significance of Homer's
works when he remarks that for the Greeks Homer was their Bible,
out of which they developed all morality.[16] In short, Hegel under-

stands Greek art, especially the epic poem, as having performed the historical function of communicating a common ethical understanding of the world; and the epic poem can therefore be thought to have had the function of orientating the actions of all the members of the historical community out of which it itself emerged.

The fact that the work of art, especially the epic poem, helped to shape the ethical world of the Greeks, as well as their conception of the divine, implies that the work of art cannot be understood in isolation from the common ethical and religious consciousness out of which it emerges and, conversely, that this ethical and religious consciousness cannot be understood in isolation from the work of art, in which both the divine and the ethical are brought more clearly to consciousness. This reciprocal relation between a work of art such as the original epic and the common religious and ethical consciousness out of which it emerges makes it easier for us to understand why Hegel speaks of the original epic as the world of a people in its totality.[17] For the original epic expresses the whole set of essential (i.e. ethical and religious) relations governing the historical community out of which it emerges. In this respect, it is not the individuality of the artist but 'the intuition of a people' that is expressed in an objective manner in the original epic,[18] with the intuition in question being a people's intuition of its own essence, that is, the set of essential relations governing its world.

What Hegel has to say of the work of art in general is therefore especially true of the original epic: it is a way and means of bringing before man what he himself is, thus satisfying his need to have what he is in general as the object of his consciousness.[19] The original epic makes possible, in short, a kind of collective self-consciousness on the part of the historical community of which it is the expression, thus allowing the transition to be made from the stage of its having an indistinct form of consciousness to the stage in this people's history at which it begins to gain self-knowledge. Moreover, the epic poet must be thought to stand in a necessary relation to that which he portrays, since the epic poem expresses the set of essential relations governing the thoughts and actions of the poet himself as well as the thoughts and actions of the other members of the historical community to which he belongs and of which the original epic is the highest expression.

Since Hegel thinks that at one point in history art had the function of mediating both ethical and religious ideas, and was, moreover, the highest form in which such ideas could be communicated, he is led to ask whether art must lose this function under changed cultural and historical conditions; and it is evident from some remarks that he makes concerning the modern epic that he thinks this to be the case. We now need to turn to Hegel's understanding of romantic art in order to identify more closely the different cultural and historical conditions under which the modern epic stands, thus preventing it from having the same kind of ethical significance as the original epic.

Hegel closely associates romantic art with Christian art, and he even refers to them as if they were essentially the same thing,[20] even though, as we shall shortly see, he thinks that art has, in more recent times, become largely independent of the Christian religion. The connection that Hegel makes between Christianity and romantic art is a reflection of the way in which he identifies the latter, broadly speaking, with Western art as it has developed since the advent of Christianity and the dissolution of the ancient world. The advent of Christianity can be seen to have two major implications for our understanding of the modern epic.

To begin with, in the wake of the advent and increasing dominance of the Christian religion, romantic art no longer appears to be the primary means of clarifying and sustaining a common ethical and religious understanding of the world; for society now finds its religious ideas and ethical norms expressed in the teachings of this historical religion. If we restrict ourselves to understanding the transition from a religion of art to the revealed religion of Christianity in purely cultural-historical terms, that is, without reference to the way in which the revealed religion is, for Hegel, closer to the 'absolute knowing' of philosophy than art, his position is essentially reducible to the following claim: the advent and increasing dominance of the Christian religion led to the latter becoming, in Europe at least, the primary source of a whole historical community's understanding of itself, as expressed in the various beliefs and norms orientating its members' thoughts and actions.

In the previous chapter we saw, moreover, that Hegel thinks that the ethical norms orientating individuals' actions have become ever more adequately embodied in laws and social institutions in the course of human history, with his own theory of modern ethical life representing his attempt to give definitive expression to how this process has achieved its full realization in the modern nation state.

This development again signals that art in the modern world stands under a wholly different set of cultural and historical conditions as compared to the set of conditions under which the original epic stood. Indeed, according to Hegel, in the case of the latter the relations of ethical life had not yet developed to the point of becoming laws, so that the sense of right and what is the proper thing to do was present only as custom.[21] It is in fact for this very reason that the original epic assumes the role of making these norms publicly available, in order that one might better know what they are and might more easily pass them on to others.

From what has been said above, it can be seen that while the original epic is universal in character because it communicates a common ethical and religious understanding of the world, as opposed to one that pertains only to particular individuals or groups within society, romantic art need not have this universal character. The independence of art in relation to ethics and religion becomes most apparent once art has freed itself from the content of the Christian religion, which previously formed its subject matter. This brings me to the second implication that the advent of Christianity has for Hegel's understanding of the differences between the modern epic and its counterpart in the ancient world.

For Hegel, the relation between romantic art and the Christian religion was initially one that turned on the way in which the former took as its subject matter the 'divine reconciliation' represented by the story of the life of Jesus, which, together with the doctrine of the Trinity, forms the distinctive content of the revealed religion.[22] However, in addition to portraying events from the life of Jesus, Hegel thinks that Christianity also makes its presence felt in romantic art in less obvious ways, so that its influence appears even in what might be seen as purely secular works of art. For romantic art can be understood to reflect the new principle which Christianity introduced into the world: the principle of subjective freedom. As we shall now see, this has some important implications with regard to our understanding of the romantic artist's relation to the content of his art.

As we already know, the right of subjective freedom, which falls under the principle of subjective freedom, constitutes a fundamental difference between antiquity and the modern age. Hegel claims, moreover, that it is in Christianity that this right is expressed 'in its infinity', and has thus become 'the universal and actual principle of a new form of the world', with love, the romantic and the salvation of the individual being specific shapes that this principle has assumed.[23] An important distinction between the ancient and the modern world thus turns out to be the greater value accorded to the individual's particularity with respect to the content of art. To begin with, and still in an obvious relation to the teachings of the Christian religion, it is such personal experiences as the individual's conversion to the Christian religion and the overcoming of sin that form the content of romantic art, as, for example, in paintings portraying Christian martyrs or saints.[24] Romantic art then develops in a way that appears to make it independent of the teachings of Christianity altogether, though it remains an expression of the principle of subjective freedom, since its content involves such themes as personal honour, romantic love and a sense of loyalty.[25] For in each case, the content of art relates to what are, for Hegel, essentially subjective features, since they have their basis in feeling and other purely contingent factors, as when, for example, individuals choose to identify their honour with one aspect of existence rather than another, or when an individual falls in love with a person whom he or she might never have chanced to meet. Another example of the way in which the principle of subjective freedom makes its presence felt in romantic art concerns the increasing importance assumed by individual character, as in Shakespeare's plays.[26]

This development results in a fundamental difference between romantic art and the art of classical Greece because, as we saw in the case of the original epic, the Greek artist stands in a necessary relation to that which he portrays, in the sense that the content of his art concerns the set of essential relations governing the thoughts and actions of all the members of the ethical world to which he himself belongs. The Greek artist therefore not only portrays a content of universal significance, but also adopts as the content of his art one that stands in a necessary relation to himself. In the case of romantic art, by contrast, this necessary connection between the artist and the content of the work of art no longer exists because of the arbitrary nature of this content, the adoption of which depends, to varying degrees, on the romantic artist's freely made decision to focus on one aspect of existence rather than another. This greater freedom with respect to the particular content of art can be understood as a reflection of the greater freedom, in the sense of the capacity to make arbitrary choices, enjoyed by modern individuals.

According to Hegel, the essentially arbitrary nature of the content of romantic art, and the way in which this content serves as the vehicle for expressing the artist's own subjectivity, reaches its logical conclusion in the writings of his contemporary, the humorist Jean-Paul Richter (1763–1825), since the material here becomes entirely subject to the ideas of the humorist; so that no content is any longer respected but is instead employed and disarranged by the arbitrary will of the subject (i.e. the humorist).[27]

The development which romantic art undergoes involves, in short, an ever weaker, in the sense of more contingent, relation between the artist and the content of the work of art, and, as we have seen, this is due to the increasing independence of art in relation to both ethics and religion. We may therefore attribute to Hegel the view that art has come to lack the higher interest which he himself demands of it.[28] He does not claim, however, that art is of no interest whatsoever in the modern world, or that it has exhausted all the possibilities open to it. In the case of the novel, which he describes as our modern epic, Hegel remarks in fact that the human dimension is the most interesting thing,[29] thus suggesting that the novel will still be of interest to modern individuals because it makes humanity into the object of art. Hegel nevertheless denies that this human dimension can have the same kind of universal significance that he accords the original epic, as the following passage makes clear:

> The novel has as its foundation a situation in which the main moments of ethical life are fixed, where ethical life no longer rests on the arbitrary will, whose range of activity is now restricted. This meagre range of activity concerns the particular interests of an individual in general, the standpoint which individuals adopt in the world.[30]

From this description of the content of the novel, it seems that the latter is concerned with the subjective aspects of human existence, which are of an essentially contingent nature. Unlike the poet in the case of the original epic, the writer of the modern epic does not therefore adopt a content that expresses, as a totality, the spirit of the historical community to which he belongs, but instead, like the romantic artist in general, chooses to focus on certain aspects of existence at the expense of others. Consequently, Hegel does not consider the interest which the modern epic has for us to be on a par with the ethically and religiously significant content that forms the subject matter of the original epic; yet this does not imply that the modern epic is for him devoid of any significance or interest whatsoever.

While the idea of the end of art cannot in Hegel's case be identified with the radical claim that art is dead, his understanding of the end of art, that is, its being unable to perform its highest function in the modern world, clearly rests on the claim that the Christian religion has taken over the historical function of mediating religious and ethical truth. The revealed religion of Christianity thus constitutes for Hegel the highest form of human knowledge apart from philosophy. We shall see, moreover, that Hegel's understanding of the significance and truth of the Christian religion is linked to an attempt on his part to show that this historical religion is compatible with human freedom. Hegel did not always view the Christian religion in this way, however. In fact, when he first began to consider the problem as to how freedom might be realized in the modern world, he held the Christian religion to be an obstacle to freedom because of its 'positivity'.

3. CHRISTIANITY AND THE PROBLEM OF 'POSITIVITY'

Among Hegel's earliest writings, first published many years after his death, is an essay entitled *The Positivity of the Christian Religion*. The term 'positivity' derives from the notion of positive law, which concerns the particular legal statutes that happen to be in force in a given legal and political community at any one time. Positive laws may be seen to rest on authority alone, in the sense that one may recognize the necessity of acting in accordance with them (e.g. through fear of punishment) while lacking any insight into their normative foundations, that is to say, into that which provides these laws with legitimacy. As we shall see below, Hegel thinks that it is also possible for individuals to act in conformity with moral and religious rules simply because they are commanded to do so, with the result that these rules come to have a positive character.

In *The Positivity of the Christian Religion*, which is mainly concerned with the role of the Christian Church in relation to its members and the state, Hegel describes how it was that the Christian religion turned into a positive religion, even though Jesus had originally sought to introduce a religion that would overcome the positivity of Judaism. In the case of the latter, daily life was, according to Hegel, governed by a host of statutory commands that prescribed rules for every casual action of daily life. There were, for example, rules prescribing how food should be prepared or on what day a certain activity might be performed. All these rules were considered to be of the same type as the civil laws governing external actions, even though many of them related to moral and religious matters, which properly belong to the individual's inner life.

The way in which the norms governing the individual's moral and religious life came to have a positive character thus had the effect of reducing morality and religion to a set of external actions performed in accordance with prescribed rules, while the disposition with which an individual performed these actions was considered to be of no importance. In other words, it did not matter whether or not a person believed that what he or she was doing was really right or holy, as long as his or her external actions were in harmony with the rules governing the moral and religious life of the Jewish people. For Hegel, this reduction of moral duty and religion to a set of rule-governed external actions amounted to nothing more than a 'mechanical slavery'.[31] Moreover, the rules in question, which had the character of legal statutes, derived their authority merely from the alleged fact that they were the revealed will of God, thus reducing both morality and religion to matters of blind obedience.

If the Christian religion was not originally, like Judaism, a positive one, the question arises as to how it became so. Hegel's answer to this question is that Jesus was forced to accommodate his teachings to the conditions of the time and the spirit of the people to whom he preached his message. Since a positive form of religion dominated the condition and spirit in question, Jesus was led to seek acceptance for his teachings by basing them on the authority of his own person, an authority which derived from his divinity, as proclaimed in his identification of himself as the Messiah and as testified through the performance of miracles. Hegel describes the consequences of Jesus' attempt to accommodate his teaching to the conditions and spirit of the age as follows:

> The result of this was to make reason a purely receptive faculty, instead of a legislative one, to make whatever could be proved to be the teaching of Jesus or, later, of his vicars, an object of reverence purely and simply because it was the teaching of Jesus or God's will, and something bound up with salvation or damnation.[32]

The way in which Hegel in this passage contrasts reason as a purely receptive faculty with reason as a legislative faculty brings to mind Kant's idea of moral autonomy, which involves an act of self-legislation, as opposed to an obedience to laws which cannot be regarded as the product of an individual's own activity. The reduction of reason to a purely receptive faculty was not, however, what Jesus originally intended; for, according to Hegel, he sought 'to raise religion and virtue to morality and to restore to morality the freedom which is its essence'.[33] This claim again reflects the influence of Kant, who makes a distinction between natural religion and revealed religion.

According to Kant, in the case of natural religion I must first know that something is a duty before I can acknowledge it as a divine command, whereas in the case of revealed religion I must first know something is a divine command in order to recognize it as my duty.[34] In other words, natural religion requires insight into the normative foundations of the moral or religious commands that I obey, whereas revealed religion treats them as commands that I must simply obey. Revealed religion thus has the character of a positive religion based on an authority that is merely given (i.e. the will of God), with the result that morality is reduced to a matter of performing actions that outwardly conform with commands that are proclaimed to reveal the will of God. Natural religion, by contrast, is a form of religion in which it is incumbent on the individual to discover for him- or herself what duty is. In other words, each individual must be convinced through the use of his or her own reason of the truth of the religious teachings which are the source of one's various duties.

Kant believes that natural religion and revealed religion are not necessarily incompatible with each other, since a revealed religion can be shown to be in accordance with natural religion if 'it is so constituted that human beings *could and ought to have* arrived at it on their own through the mere use of their reason'.[35] In other words, the teachings of a revealed religion may in fact accord with natural religion, even though it is better for individuals to first discover the truths of natural religion, so that they might judge the teachings of revealed religion in the light of them. In this respect, the relation of revealed religion to natural religion is analogous to the relation between positive law and natural law, which in Kant's and Hegel's time was taken to include the normative foundations of law in general, in so far as insight into these normative foundations was to provide the standard by means of which positive laws were to be judged. For Kant, it is morality that provides the normative foundations for any revealed religion that may justifiably claim to be in harmony with reason as a self-legislating faculty. He thinks, moreover, that the teachings of Jesus are a case in point, since many of them correspond to genuine duties to which the moral subject may freely subject itself.

In the light of Kant's distinction between natural and revealed religion, we may take Hegel's point to be that Jesus originally intended to teach a natural form of religion, that is, a religion into which individuals could gain rational insight and thus recognize the moral demands that it makes on them as being ones that they ought to make their own by developing the disposition to act in accordance with them, rather than their simply following commands that have the character of legal statutes. The fact that Jesus was forced to accommodate his teachings to the prevailing conditions and spirit of the age meant, however, that all moral duties came to derive their authority from his own person and not from the fact that they were in themselves duties.

This invites the question as to whether the Christian religion might be purged of its positivity by once again making morality into its essence, as Jesus originally intended. On the whole, Hegel appears to be highly sceptical regarding such a possibility in *The Positivity of the Christian Religion*; for in this early work he stresses the various ways in which, throughout its history, the Christian religion has tended to take on a positive form. He claims, in fact, that whereas Judaism commanded only actions, the Christian Church even commands feelings (e.g. repentance, pious fervour). Yet the idea of commanding feelings is a contradiction in terms, since feelings cannot be produced at will; and Hegel therefore argues that it was impossible for the Christian Church to produce anything more in this way than 'legality and a mechanical virtue and piety'.[36]

Hegel's views on the positivity of the Christian religion invite the idea that it serves as the epitome of an object which, in its mere givenness, confronts the individual as something alien that nevertheless dominates him.[37] Yet he later came to call the Christian religion the religion of truth and freedom.[38] This apparent change in attitude towards the Christian religion seems all the more remarkable given the fact that, in *The Positivity of the Christian Religion*, Hegel com-

pares the unfreedom of the Christian religion unfavourably with the
political freedom enjoyed by the citizens of the Greek city-state and
the Roman Republic. For Hegel, the citizens of the Greek city-state
and the Roman Republic were free because they 'obeyed laws laid
down by themselves, obeyed men whom they had themselves
appointed to office' and 'waged wars on which they had themselves
decided'.[39] In short, the citizens of the Greek city-state and the
Roman Republic were free because they performed acts of self-legislation rather than merely obeying positive commands. Consequently,
the Greek or Roman citizen could identify himself with the state and
was ready to sacrifice his own life on its behalf because it was his own
work and that which gave meaning to his life. Hegel claims, moreover,
that the Greek and Roman religions were religions for free people
because they had an integral role to play in relation to the state, which
formed the end of the individual citizen's activity, as when the gods
were taken to bestow gifts vital to political life, such as wisdom and
eloquence, or when they were consulted with regard to whether a pro-
posed undertaking would turn out well or badly.

The citizen's act of identifying the state as his own highest end was
made more difficult, however, by certain developments that took
place in the Roman world, namely, the ceding of political power to a
particular group of people (i.e. the aristocracy) and then to a single
individual (i.e. the Roman Emperor), together with an increase in
wealth and luxury. This resulted in a condition in which the citizens
of the Empire were no longer able to recognize the state as the product
of their own activity, and it came to have for them the purely instrumental function of protecting their own persons and property. Just as
political freedom went together with a religion for a free people, this
loss of political freedom became associated with a religion that
reflected this loss: one that worships a transcendent God placed
beyond the boundaries of human power, a God towards which
human beings stand in a merely passive relation, and to which they
are willing to cede all legislation. Moreover, death no longer had the
meaning that it had when one willingly sacrificed one's own life for an
end (i.e. the state) with which one fully identified oneself. The com-
forting belief in personal immortality therefore became necessary,
and human beings thus came to seek and expect happiness in heaven,
not on earth.

As we saw in the previous chapter, the kind of privatism which
Hegel associates with the Christian religion in *The Positivity of the*

Christian Religion, along with the loss of political freedom in the sense of direct political participation, are features of the modern state as presented in his philosophy of right. This suggests that Hegel did not come to think of the Christian religion as the religion of truth and freedom because it could serve as a public religion that was essentially bound up with the political freedom and political activity of the members of the modern state. In what sense, then, does Hegel understand the Christian religion to be the religion of truth and freedom?

The short answer to this question is that Hegel came to develop an account of the Christian religion which he believed shows that it accords with the principle of subjective freedom because the subjective aspect of faith forms an essential element of the Christian religion, thus making the latter compatible with the right of the subject to experience the satisfaction of its particularity and to identify itself with the objects of its concern. However, as we shall see below, Hegel also thinks that the subjective aspect of faith needs to be supplemented by a determinate content, the truth of which can be demonstrated by means of a philosophy of religion. In other words, the content of the Christian faith must be shown to be compatible with the right of individuals to have an insight into what they hold to be good or true; for it is the possibility of gaining rational insight into this content that allows the positivity, which still characterizes the Christian religion as a revealed religion, to be fully overcome.

In order to understand why Hegel later came to call the Christian religion the religion of truth and freedom, we therefore need to turn to his account of the essential nature of Christian faith and its subjective dimension in particular, which concerns the right of the subject to experience the satisfaction of its particularity and to identify itself with the objects of its concern. Hegel's criticisms of a subjectivist conception of faith for being one-sided will then lead us to consider the content of faith, which constitutes its objective dimension, and Hegel's attempt to explain the possibility of gaining rational insight into the content of the Christian religion.

4. HEGEL'S ACCOUNT OF FAITH

A good example of a subjectivist conception of the essence of religious faith is to be found in the thought of Søren Kierkegaard (1813–1855), who is often taken to be one of Hegel's earliest critics.

Kierkegaard makes the following uncompromising statement concerning Christian faith in particular: 'Christianity is spirit; spirit is inwardness; inwardness is subjectivity; subjectivity is essentially passion, and at its maximum an infinite, personally interested passion for one's eternal happiness'.[40] Christian faith is here first identified with inwardness, as opposed to any features of the Christian religion, such as its doctrines and the institutions of the Church, which are understood to possess an authority that makes them independent of the individual believer's personal response to the teachings of this historical religion. Inwardness is then identified with a feeling, passion; and the essentially subjective nature of feeling means that Kierkegaard's description of the passionate interest in one's eternal happiness as a purely personal one is to the point.

One implication of this subjectivist conception of faith is that although I might seek to communicate such a feeling of religious conviction to others, who may well be able to understand in a formal sense what I mean, these others may not themselves experience the very same feeling that I experience. For Kierkegaard, since passion is the essential thing in religious faith, and such passion cannot be expressed in objective terms, it is wholly inappropriate to attempt to communicate one's personal religious experiences in the same way as one seeks to communicate a fact about the world.[41] In short, religious faith is essentially a matter of inwardness.

In his lectures on the philosophy of religion, Hegel claims that an appeal to one's own feelings 'breaks off the commonality between us', whereas in the case of thought or the concept 'we meet one another on the soil of the universal, of rationality'.[42] Given the connection that Hegel elsewhere makes between rationality and autonomy, this assessment of the limits of feeling may appear to suggest a purely negative attitude on his part to the kind of subjectivist conception of faith that Kierkegaard adopts, a conception of faith which stresses its ultimate incommunicability. We shall shortly see, however, that Hegel holds a feeling of religious conviction to be an essential moment of faith and that he seeks to provide a vital link between it and reason in the case of the Christian religion. We should therefore be cautious about taking Hegel's account of the limitations of feeling to constitute an outright rejection of the kind of religious subjectivism which we find in Kierkegaard's account of the essence of faith. In what follows, we shall see in fact that this kind of religious subjectivism is, in spite of its one-sidedness, an expression of the principle of subjective freedom, which for Hegel is a distinctive feature of the modern world.

Hegel encountered such a subjectivist conception of the essence of faith in his own time in the thought of Friedrich Heinrich Jacobi (1743–1819), and in this respect Kierkegaard can be viewed as belonging to a well-established tradition. Hegel's attitude to such religious subjectivism is in fact a complex one; for although he thinks that it captures an essential aspect of genuine Christian faith, he also views it as giving rise to a significant problem with regard to the content of faith. As far as the positive dimension to Hegel's account of the subjective aspect of faith is concerned, this relates to the way in which the subject experiences the satisfaction of its particularity because, as this specific individual, he or she feels personally convinced of the truth of the object of faith.

Hegel is nevertheless critical of the kind of religious subjectivism which he associates with Jacobi on account of its failure to establish a meaningful link between such inherently subjective features as a feeling of conviction and the doctrines which serve to distinguish Christianity from other historical religions. For instance, to use Kierkegaard's characterization of Christianity as an example, there does not appear to be an obvious link between a passionate interest in one's eternal happiness and the Christian religion in particular, as opposed to any of the other historical religions that hold out the promise of eternal happiness. This problem is one that Hegel himself raises in connection with Jacobi's idea of an 'immediate knowing' which 'asserts that God and the true can only be known immediately'.[43] We therefore need to look briefly at Hegel's attitude to this form of knowing in so far as it can be viewed as a religious form of consciousness.

Jacobi's reduction of our knowledge of God to faith or immediate knowing rests, for Hegel, on the mistaken idea that thinking is always a finite activity which is incapable of grasping the infinite; for thinking is here understood to always involve a cognition which proceeds sequentially from one conditioned item to another, with each conditioned item itself being conditioned, or mediated, by something else. In other words, thought is restricted to seeking to discover the causal connections which determine the relations of finite entities to each other. It thus fails to grasp the truth of that which lies outside this set of causal relations and constitutes its condition. Consequently, every content is for this type of thinking only a '*particular*, *dependent*, and *finite* one', whereas 'God, or what is infinite and true, lies outside the mechanism of a connection of this kind to which cognition is supposed to be restricted'.[44] In other words, God is not to be understood as one entity within the world among others; the concept of God instead expresses a content that is of an entirely different kind from any finite entity. Yet immediate knowing's attempt to comprehend God without turning the latter into one finite entity among others ends up reducing God to something wholly indeterminate, as we shall now see.

In his account of immediate knowing, Hegel clearly has in mind Jacobi's claim that reason is only able to uncover new conditions for what is conditioned, with these new conditions in turn being conditioned by further conditions, whereas God lies outside the mechanism which determines the relations of finite entities to each other. Jacobi then argues that our representations of the conditioned must presuppose the representation of the unconditioned, which is the condition of the possibility of the existence of the temporal world or nature, in the sense that the latter, as a complex of conditioned things, must be grounded in something supernatural which lies outside it. According to Jacobi, we are therefore as certain of the existence of the unconditioned as we are of the existence of the external world. However, since reason can directly encounter only the complex of conditioned beings that constitutes nature, from which reason ultimately derives all its concepts, the unconditioned cannot be apprehended by us except as a given fact, which finds expression in the words 'it is'; and this is what all tongues proclaim as God.[45]

Jacobi's claim that the unconditioned is expressed in the words 'it is', and the way in which he identifies this 'it is' with God, leads Hegel to argue that since it extends only to the assertion '*that* God is, not *what* God is', the immediate knowing of God expressly limits the object of religion to '*God in general*, to the indeterminate supersensible'.[46] Hegel's main criticism of Jacobi's conception of God can therefore be seen to rest on the idea that by identifying God with the statement 'it is', Jacobi fails to specify any determinate features that might serve to distinguish the God which forms the object of Christian faith from other conceptions of God, such as the abstract one which the symbolic form of art unsuccessfully attempts to express in sensory form. The simple assertion of the fact that God exists does not, in short, provide us with a determinate representation of God. In the following passage, Hegel, by contrast, seeks to distinguish genuine Christian faith from the faith of immediate knowing, which restricts the content of religion to God in general:

> The Christian faith implies an authority that belongs to the church, while, on the contrary, the faith of this philosophising standpoint is just the authority of one's own subjective revelation. Moreover, the Christian faith is an objective content that is inwardly rich, a system of doctrine and cognition; whereas the content of this [philosophical] faith is inwardly so indeterminate that it may perhaps admit that content too – but equally it may embrace within it the belief that the Dalaï-Lama, the bull, the ape, etc., is God, or it may, for its own part, restrict itself to God in general, to the 'highest essence'.[47]

In this passage, Hegel stresses the importance of the doctrinal content that serves to distinguish the Christian religion from other historical religions, so as to make a clear distinction between true faith and the faith of immediate knowing, which in his view fails to provide a determinate representation of God. The reference to subjective revelation suggests, moreover, that Hegel thinks of immediate knowing as involving a subjectivist conception of faith that reduces the latter to a matter of feeling. Indeed, he elsewhere states that the immediate knowledge, or rather conviction, that God exists, makes feeling into the ground of our knowledge of God's being.[48] This appears to accord with Jacobi's own view of the matter; for even though he speaks of an intuition of reason, which makes us certain of the actuality and truth of certain supersensible objects, he claims that this intuition is given us in feelings of rapture, and that it is based on the authority of the feeling of the spirit.[49]

Since the subjective certainty that God exists fails to provide a determinate representation of God, Hegel argues that feeling is 'a *mere form*, indeterminate on its own account and capable of holding any content whatever'.[50] In the absence of a determinate representation of God, which is, moreover, held to possess an authority that makes it independent of the believer's subjective state of belief, the individual's feelings and convictions come to decide what is to count as religious truth; yet, as Hegel points out, this turns knowledge of God into a matter of caprice.

This problem of indeterminacy with regard to the representation of God is thus understood by Hegel to be related to the tendency to base faith on religious feeling alone. Since Hegel thinks that the kind of subjectivist conception of religious faith that Jacobi has to offer does not imply a specifically Christian type of faith, he attempts to offer a more adequate account of the latter by describing it as follows:

> . . . I understand by faith neither the merely subjective state of belief which is restricted to the form of certainty, leaving untouched the nature of the content, if any, of the belief, nor on the other hand only the *credo*, the church's confession of faith which can be recited and learnt by rote without communicating itself to man's innermost self, without being identified with the certainty which a man has of himself, with his consciousness of himself. I hold that faith, in the true, ancient sense of the word, is a unity of both these moments, including the one no less than the other.[51]

In this passage, Hegel clearly identifies two essential moments of religious faith: on the one hand, there is the individual's conviction that he is a witness to religious truth, and, on the other hand, there is religious doctrine, which possesses an authority that makes it independent of the particular feelings, opinions and convictions of the individual believer. In other words, Hegel's concept of religious faith contains two different senses of the word faith: the subjective state of feeling convinced that the object of one's faith is the truth and *the* faith, that is, a determinate body of doctrines and teachings which is believed to possess an authority that makes it independent of what any single individual holds to be the true content of religion.

Hegel's concept of faith implies that while he identifies the subjective side of faith with a type of certainty that is as strong as the certainty that one has of one's own existence, this certainty is at the same time directed towards an object which is held to possess an absolute authority that makes it independent of the subjective state of the individual believer; so that the object in question is, as Hegel himself puts it, 'not merely something subjective but is also an absolute, objective content that is in and for itself, and has the characteristic of truth'.[52] By stressing the unity of the two moments of faith in the way that he does, Hegel shows that he wants to reconcile the inwardness of faith with the kind of objective content found in religious doctrine, rather than privileging one moment of faith in relation to the other. Once the objective moment of faith has communicated itself to an individual's own innermost self, which it must do if the subjective moment of faith is to be present, thus overcoming the problem of positivity, the individual concerned will identify him- or herself with the object of faith in the sense that the truth of the latter is not grounded on an external authority alone, but is instead also validated by this individual's own inner conviction of its truth.

Religious feeling therefore guarantees that each individual, as this specific individual, identifies him- or herself with the content of faith (i.e. religious doctrine), and thus experiences the satisfaction of his or her particularity, because the content of faith is validated by that which is of an essentially subjective nature. The importance that Hegel attaches to the subjective aspect of religious faith is evident from his claim that the 'witness of the spirit', as opposed to miracles and historical verification, is 'the absolutely proper ground of belief, the absolute testimony to the content of a religion'.[53] Consequently, he treats miracles and historical fact as being inessential to religious faith; and, as we shall see, this forms an important part of his attempt to demonstrate the implicit rationality of the content of the Christian religion.

While the right to experience the satisfaction of one's particularity is met in the case of genuine religious faith through the feeling of being personally convinced that the object of one's faith is the absolute truth, the question arises as to what is the ultimate basis of this unity of the subjective and objective moments of faith. Given Hegel's views on the inherently subjective and indeterminate nature of feeling, it is clear that he does not consider it to be the only basis of the unity in question; and the importance that he attaches to the task of demonstrating the implicit rationality of the content of the Christian religion here comes into play. Hegel has two interconnected reasons for seeking to explain the unity of the subjective and objective moments of faith in terms of the implicit rationality of the content of the Christian religion, the first of which is an historical one, while the second concerns the concept of autonomy. In order to understand what the historical reason is, we need to turn to Hegel's thoughts on the relation between faith and the Enlightenment, as represented by such figures of the French Enlightenment as Voltaire and D'Holbach, who were highly critical of the claims of all historical religions, especially those of Christianity.

5. FAITH AND THE ENLIGHTENMENT

According to Hegel, the Enlightenment was not initially hostile to religion. It was instead hostile only to the way in which the human understanding gave a fixed and settled meaning to the body of narratives and teachings that provide faith with its content (i.e. religious doctrine), and then attempted to set up this body of narratives and teachings as a canon of belief for others, with the result that their understanding became subject to the understanding which wanted to set up these canons of belief and demands subjection to them in the name of divine truth.[54] In other words, the officials of the Christian church turned the teachings of the Christian religion into a fixed body of doctrines, which the laity was expected simply to accept as being true on these officials' authority. The Christian religion was, in short, turned into a positive religion. Hegel therefore thinks that part of the historical importance of the Enlightenment concerns the way in which it turned against the setting up of an external authority in religious matters and thus asserted the right of the subject to have an insight into what it holds to be good or true.

Hegel also sees the importance of the Enlightenment as lying in its attack upon the tendency of religious faith to turn the divine truth into something finite, as is evident from the following passage:

> Thus its intention at first was to attack error and superstition and, indeed, what it truly succeeded in destroying was not religion, but that pharisaical mentality which had applied the wisdom of this world to the things of another world and fancied that its sophistries could also be called religious doctrine. It wanted to remove error solely to make room for the Truth.[55]

In other words, the Enlightenment attacks the way in which the Christian Church accords certain images, objects and relations drawn from finite experience an absolute status, as if they were essential to religion, and then demands for them the same reverence and faith as for that which forms the true content of religion. As we shall see, Hegel himself makes a clear distinction between the historical claims of the Christian religion, which for him relate only to the appearance of the divine truth, and the latter as it is in itself.

In its attempt to purge religion of all elements deriving from superstition, the Enlightenment proceeds in a purely negative manner, however, since it restricts itself to demonstrating the merely temporal and finite character of the historical narratives and fixed images that have become associated with the divine truth. For Hegel, this activity on the part of the Enlightenment means that while it is able to restore and assert the freedom of spirit, it fails to distinguish between a merely finite content and the truth itself. The Enlightenment is, in fact, able to demonstrate the incommensurability of any finite content with the divine truth only by depriving the latter of all content whatsoever. Consequently, the Enlightenment's critique of religion deprives religion of 'a truth that is *known*, an *objective content*, a *doctrinal* theology'.[56] Yet, as we have seen, Hegel does not think that this loss of content can be remedied by an appeal to an immediate knowing which has its basis in feeling alone. Indeed, he shows that this immediate knowing empties religion of all content equally as much as the Enlightenment critique of religion does.

The tension between Enlightenment reason and religious faith forms the subject matter of part of the section on culture in the *Phenomenology of Spirit*. Hegel claims that the Enlightenment has 'the *intention* of making *pure insight universal*, i.e. of making everything that is actual into a concept, and into one and the same concept in every self-consciousness'.[57] In other words, the Enlightenment seeks to comprehend all reality in terms of universal determinations (i.e. concepts), and, since all individuals must be thought to share in common the same essential nature in so far as they are rational, everyone will be capable of recognizing the validity of these determinations. It is this fixation on universality that leads Hegel to characterize the principle of the Enlightenment as one of pure insight; and it is against religious faith that the pure insight of the Enlightenment directs its conceptual grasp of reality. It does so by seeking to expose the errors and lies of religion, as when it claims that religion is a deception contrived by a priesthood which claims to possess a privileged knowledge of the divine, or when it attacks faith for treating finite objects, such as images carved out of wood, as if they were divine. The Enlightenment also criticizes faith for its dependence on historical narratives, the accuracy of which is open to doubt; and we here again encounter what will turn out to be an important feature of Hegel's attempt to demonstrate the implicit rationality of the Christian religion, so as to defend it against the Enlightenment critique of religion, namely, his rejection of the idea that the truth of the Christian religion rests on historical fact.

Hegel claims that the Enlightenment misconstrues the essence of faith, however; for as far as the priesthood's alleged deception of the masses is concerned, he asks how it is possible for the religious consciousness to be so completely deceived about what it takes to be its very essence? While, in the case of faith's treatment of finite objects as something divine, Hegel claims that it is the Enlightenment itself which, as he puts it, 'converts what is for Spirit eternal life and Holy Spirit into an actual, *perishable thing*, and defiles it with sense-certainty's view of it, a viewpoint which is essentially trivial and definitely absent from faith in its worship'.[58] Finally, as far as its dependence on historical narratives is concerned, Hegel states that rather than seeking its basis in such narratives, for the religious consciousness 'it is Spirit itself which bears witness to itself'.[59] In short, it seems that for Hegel the Enlightenment makes the mistake of trying to comprehend religious faith in terms that are alien to faith's own understanding of itself. The fact that Hegel thinks that genuine Christian faith does not rely on historical narratives, as the Enlightenment thinks it does, will, however, lead me to question whether he himself does not end up comprehending faith in terms that are alien to its own understanding of itself.

In spite of misconstruing the essential nature of religious faith in the way that it does, the Enlightenment is nevertheless an expression of the demand of self-conscious reason to have insight into what it holds to be good or true, a demand that is essential to Hegel's own attempt to explain how autonomy is possible in the modern world. Consequently, if the principle of subjective freedom is to be fully realized in the case of the Christian religion, the conflict between faith and reason must be resolved; yet this will require explaining the possibility of gaining rational insight into the content of religious faith. For Hegel, the unity of the subjective and objective moments of faith must, in other words, be rooted in human reason, rather than being based solely on feeling, which represents an essentially subjective and therefore contingent source of justification. The central teachings of Christian religion must, in short, be shown to be compatible with the highly reflective type of thought whose highest manifestation is philosophy. This brings me to Hegel's philosophy of religion and his attempt to show, through a critique of religious representational thought, that the content of the Christian religion is essentially the same as the content of philosophy.

6. HEGEL'S CRITIQUE OF RELIGIOUS REPRESENTATIONAL THOUGHT

The need to go beyond the standpoint of religion itself to that of a philosophy of religion is due to the inherent limitations of the form (i.e. representational thought) in which the content that the Christian religion shares in common with philosophy is present to the religious consciousness. The critical dimension to Hegel's account of religious representational thought is evident from the way in which he defines the latter largely in terms of the limitations from which it suffers in comparison to the purely conceptual type of thought that constitutes the form of knowledge in the case of philosophy. These limitations are as follows:

1. Religious representational thought contains what can generally be termed images which have an 'inner' meaning, since they have an allegorical or symbolic function.[60] For instance, the representation that God has begotten a son (i.e. Christ) is a metaphor drawn from the world of everyday experience that nevertheless manages to express a transition which philosophy is able to comprehend in purely conceptual terms. The allegorical or symbolical elements contained in such a representation prevent God from being comprehended as he is in himself, however.

2. Religious representational thought presents the eternal truth in an historical shape and thereby ends up containing what can be regarded as two conflicting elements: the eternal or divine and the finite. For instance, according to Hegel, the story of Jesus is something 'twofold' because it not only contains an 'outward history', which is only 'the ordinary story of a human being', but also has the divine as its content; yet it is only this divine element which is 'the inward, the genuine, the substantial dimension of this history, and . . . the object of reason'.[61] Hegel thus downplays the importance of historical fact in relation to the question of the truth of the Christian religion.

3. Religious representational thought fails to exhibit the necessity underlying its various determinations, which are therefore

merely linked together in an external fashion, as when God is characterized as being omniscient, omnipotent, infinitely just, and so on. This leaves us with a set of fixed determinations, each of which is simple and remains independent alongside other determinations, so that their combination depends on the words 'and' and 'also', which link these determinations together in an external fashion.[62]

In contrast, philosophy comprehends the content of religion in purely conceptual terms and is thus able to purge the doctrines of Christianity of any remaining sensuous or historical features and to exhibit the necessity of the various moments of these doctrines. Hegel therefore wants to offer a philosophical justification of the content of the Christian religion through a critique of its representational form of thought; and the task that he sets himself is summarized in the following passage:

> God has revealed himself through the Christian religion; that is, he has granted mankind the possibility of recognising what he is, so that he is no longer an impenetrable mystery. The fact that knowledge of God is possible also makes it our duty to know him, and that development of the thinking spirit which proceeds from this foundation, the revelation of the divine being, must eventually produce a situation in which all that was at first present to spirit in feeling and representation can also be comprehended by thought.[63]

In other words, God has revealed himself through the Christian religion but in an inadequate way. For, on the one hand, the nature of God has been revealed in religious doctrine, which for Hegel belongs to the realm of representational thought and therefore suffers from the limitations mentioned above, and, on the other hand, the content of religion is validated not by reason but by a subjective state of the believer, namely, a feeling of religious conviction. The task is therefore to comprehend the content of faith, which has thus far appeared in the form of feeling and religious representational thought, in terms of thought alone, that is, in purely conceptual terms.

Hegel's approach could, however, be cited as evidence of an essentially ambiguous relation to the Christian religion because the critical dimension to this project, which requires purging the content of the Christian religion of its images and historical features, may result in something which the religious consciousness would no longer be able to recognize as its own. In other words, just as Hegel accuses the Enlightenment of misconstruing the essential nature of religious faith, he himself might also be accused of comprehending religious faith in terms that are alien to faith's own understanding of itself, even though his aim is to justify the Christian religion rather than to undermine it. I shall shortly suggest in relation to the second of the limitations of religious representational thought listed above that this is precisely what Hegel appears to do. First, however, I need to say something more about Hegel's attempt to offer a philosophical reinterpretation of Christian doctrine.

As previously mentioned, the most important of these doctrines is the doctrine of the Trinity, which for Hegel expresses the new conception of the divine that enters the world with the Christian religion. In the section on religion in the *Encyclopaedia*, Hegel reinterprets this doctrine in terms of the logical concept, of which he gives an account in his works on logic. The logical concept has three moments: universality, particularity and individuality (or singularity).[64] Hegel understands these three moments as being necessarily related to each other, as opposed to each of them being an independent entity that can be fully understood in isolation from the other moments of the logical concept. The logical concept is, in short, a totality of interrelated determinations, that is to say, a concrete universal. We have already encountered an example of this type of universality in Chapter 2 in connection with Hegel's account of the concept of the will, which is individual in the sense that it involves the unity of the moments of universality and particularity.

To begin with, Hegel associates the person of the Father, 'creator of heaven and earth', with the first moment of the logical concept, universality; and he describes this moment of the doctrine of the Trinity as 'the sphere of pure thought or the abstract element of essence'.[65] He then associates the second person of the Trinity, the person of the Son, with the moment of particularity.[66] In connection with the transition from the first to the second person of the Trinity, Hegel claims, moreover, that the 'absolute Being which exists as an actual self-consciousness seems to have come down from its eternal simplicity, but by thus *coming down* it has in fact attained for the first time to its own highest essence'.[67] What he means by this is that even though God may appear to have become less God-like by becoming an actual self-consciousness, he nevertheless realizes himself as God in the Incarnation.

As a specific individual, Christ stands in a merely external relation to heaven and earth and finite spirit, however. As we shall see in the next chapter, this kind of external relation is a finite one for Hegel because it involves a relation in which something is limited by something else that remains essentially other than it. To use the relation of Christ to finite spirit as an example, Hegel describes the person of Christ in the *Phenomenology of Spirit* as an 'exclusive One or unit', so that 'Spirit as an individual Self is not yet equally the universal Self, the Self of everyone'.[68] The thought here seems to be that Christ, as an individual person, is present to human consciousness as one particular among others, so that his person fails to express the universal self-consciousness of spirit, which is a concrete universal because each individual self-consciousness stands in a necessary relation to others of the same general type as itself. The Incarnation does not therefore represent the unity of universality and particularity that constitutes the third moment of the concept, individuality. We instead have a merely external relation between the universal (i.e. spirit) and the particular (i.e. the person of Christ).

This kind of external relation is in fact due to one of the limitations to which Hegel thinks representational thought in general is subject: its failure to exhibit the necessity underlying its various determinations, which are therefore linked together in an external fashion. In the case of the religious representation of the Trinity, this means that the absolute unity of the universal and the particular has yet to be fully revealed to humankind. The defect in question is remedied, however, by the representation of the death of Christ and the subsequent presence of the Holy Spirit in the universal self-consciousness of the Christian community.[69] In other words, the Holy Spirit represents the overcoming of the moment of particularity and the return to universality, though this time the universal is a concrete one which contains the particular within itself; for although Christ dies as a particular individual, he is still present within the universal (i.e. the Christian community) in the shape of the Holy Spirit.

Even if we grant that Hegel has succeeded in offering a philosophical reinterpretation of the doctrine of the Trinity, the question remains as to whether his critique of religious representational thought sufficiently preserves what the religious consciousness itself takes to be essential to the truth of the Christian religion. As I now intend to show, one reason for holding that it fails to do this relates specifically to the second moment of the doctrine of the Trinity (i.e. the Incarnation) and the second of the limitations of religious representational thought listed above. For Hegel appears to think that the historical fact of the Incarnation is, from the standpoint of philosophy, an accidental feature of the Christian religion; and he thus invites the reduction of the whole life of Jesus to the status of myth as undertaken by David Friedrich Strauss (1808–1874), a follower of Hegel, in his life of Jesus. It could be argued, in fact, that Strauss is more aware than Hegel of the implications of his critique of religious representational thought, or is less cautious about stating what these implications are. Indeed, Strauss saw his rejection of the historical content of the life of Jesus, together with his claim that such a rejection does not affect the truth of Christianity, as having their source in Hegel's philosophy, especially in his distinction between representational thought and concept, a distinction which for Strauss raises the possibility of bringing respect for biblical documents and church dogmas into harmony with the freedom of thought.[70] This assessment of the potential of Hegel's distinction between representational thought and concept corresponds to Hegel's own understanding of the aim of his philosophical interpretation of the doctrine of the Trinity, which is to show how the latter accords with the right of the modern subject to have rational insight into what it holds to be good or true.

Another point on which Hegel and Strauss are clearly in agreement relates to the way in which the latter thinks there has been an advance in human thought and culture that has resulted in an increasing tension between what a people has generally come to accept as adequate evidence or marks of truth and the writings on which its religion is based.[71] For even though Hegel does not speak of a tension between human thought and religion, we have seen from his account of the relation of faith to the Enlightenment that he clearly holds the view that there has been an advance in human culture which has led to a change in what people should be prepared to accept as the marks of religious truth. Moreover, just as Hegel thinks that his philosophical reinterpretation of Christian doctrine does not serve to undermine the latter, Strauss thinks that his mythical account of the life of Jesus does not mean that the story of Jesus is devoid of all truth. He claims instead that the core beliefs of the Christian religion are independent of his critical investigations and that the events of the life of Jesus, such as his supernatural birth and his resurrection, remain eternal truths, however much their actuality as historical facts may be doubted.[72] Strauss thus downplays the importance of the historical facts of Jesus' life, just as Hegel does, while claiming that this life contains eternal truths, even though it belongs to the realm of myth. This again accords with one of the basic ideas behind Hegel's philosophy of religion: his distinction between the external (i.e. merely historical) aspects of the story of Jesus, which he attributes to the limitations of religious representational thought, and its inner truth.

Strauss identifies the inner truth of the Incarnation with the idea of humanity as a whole. For he argues in relation to the idea of the God-man, which finds concrete expression in the mythical person of Christ, that the predicates which the Church ascribes to a single individual, that is, the two natures, the finite and the infinite, or the human and the divine, are in harmony with each other only in the idea of the human race, whereas they contradict each other when predicated of Christ, who is a single individual.[73] We may here leave aside the question as to whether Strauss is really justified in claiming that the two natures are in harmony with each other in the idea of the human race, a move that appears to simply suppress one of the terms of the contradiction found in the idea of the Incarnation (i.e. the divine aspect of Christ's nature). What is significant about Strauss' position in relation to Hegel's philosophy of religion is that it largely corresponds to Hegel's own position with regard to the inner truth of the Incarnation, in spite of one important difference. The difference in question is that Hegel does not claim that the truth of the Incarnation is to be found only in the idea of the human race, that is, in the idea of the universal self-consciousness of spirit, since the Incarnation also corresponds to the logical concept. In this respect, Hegel sees the Incarnation as representing a truth that transcends the realm of finite spirit, whereas Strauss appears to identify the truth of this teaching with the latter. Nevertheless, both Hegel and Strauss offer an interpretation of the doctrine of the Incarnation that treats its historical dimension (i.e. the fact that there once existed a person called Jesus of Nazareth who really was the Son of God) as being accidental to its truth.

For both Hegel and Strauss the Incarnation does not, in short, have any basis in historical fact. Nor does it help to claim that Hegel's philosophy presupposes 'historically' that the Incarnation of God in Christ has for the Christian community already taken place.[74] For this claim is an ambiguous one, which could be taken to mean only that the representation of the Incarnation must have already entered human consciousness; an interpretation which would be compatible with the idea that the Incarnation is a product of the mythical consciousness of the early Christian community, as Strauss thinks it is. In other words, it still allows us to understand the representation of the Incarnation as being immanent to consciousness. We might, therefore, equally attribute to Hegel the view that the historical person and life of Christ are products of the collective religious consciousness of the Christian community because he thinks that the historical aspect of the Incarnation belongs only to the form in which this doctrine is present to human consciousness, but not to the true content of the Christian religion. Consequently, it is difficult not to think of Strauss' reduction of the life of the historical Jesus to the status of myth as being in harmony with Hegel's philosophy of religion, just as Strauss himself thought it was.

The fact that the belief that there once existed a person called Jesus of Nazareth who really was the Son of God appears to be incompatible with Hegel's philosophy of religion invites a left-Hegelian interpretation of the latter. When I speak of a left-Hegelian interpretation of Hegel's philosophy of religion I have in mind Strauss' claim that it was Hegel's views concerning the person and story of Christ that led the Hegel school to split into three distinct groups; a division that Strauss explains in terms of the three possible ways of answering the question whether and to what extent the gospel story of Jesus is proven to be history by Hegel's idea of the unity of the divine and human natures. The three possible ways of answering this question are as follows: either the entire gospel (right Hegelianism), or merely part of it (the centre), or neither the whole or part of it (left Hegelianism) is to be confirmed as historical by the idea of the divine–human unity.[75] In my view, Hegel's account of the Incarnation clearly implies the last of these three possible ways of answering the question whether and to what extent the gospel story of Jesus is proven to be history by his idea of the unity of the divine and human natures.

Hegel's rejection of the historical fact of the Incarnation is of particular relevance in relation to the thought of Kierkegaard, who was one of the earliest critics of Hegelianism. Kierkegaard criticizes Strauss' identification of the idea of the God-man with humanity for ignoring the infinite qualitative difference that exists between God and man.[76] In other words, Kierkegaard thinks that Strauss is able to overcome the contradiction found in the doctrine of the Incarnation only by reducing the two natures (i.e. the divine and human) to that of the human and finite, thus ignoring Christ's divinity altogether. For Kierkegaard, by contrast, the Incarnation decisively distinguishes Christianity from all other historical religions, and thus provides the basis for the distinction that he makes between religiousness A and religiousness B. While the former type of religiousness concerns the individual's infinite interest in his eternal happiness, it is not a specifically Christian form of religiousness, since in this type of religiousness the eternal is in its omnipresence both everywhere and nowhere.[77] While religiousness A can therefore be associated with paganism and immanence, religiousness B, in stark contrast, constitutes a decisive break with immanence because for it the eternal is present at a specific moment in time. The object of its faith is the absolute paradox as expressed in the thesis that 'God has existed in human form, was born, grew up etc.'[78] In other words, in the Christian religion, the Incarnation qualifies the eternal happiness which forms the object of the individual's infinite interest, since faith in the person of Christ is the condition of eternal happiness.

Kierkegaard's absolute paradox shows that for him the historical aspect of the Incarnation is an integral part of this religious doctrine, so that, in addition to objecting to the way in which Strauss reduces the idea of the God-man to the idea of humanity, he must also object to the way in which Hegel suppresses the historical aspect of the Incarnation so as to be able to comprehend it in purely conceptual terms. Kierkegaard therefore provides us with a good example as to how, from the standpoint of faith, Hegel might stand accused of misconstruing the true content of faith, which in this case involves treating the historical aspect of the teaching of the Incarnation as inessential to the Christian religion. There are, in short, grounds for arguing that Hegel's attempt to demonstrate the implicit rationality of the Christian religion comes at the price of understanding the latter in terms that are radically different from the way in which the religious consciousness itself understands the teachings of this religion.

The movement away from that which has an external presence in space and time is, however, for Hegel one that thought must make in order to fully comprehend the truth. In this respect, religion, in so far as it seeks to base itself on historical fact, as when it insists that we treat the historical aspect of the Incarnation as essential to the truth of the Christian religion, represents a step in the wrong direction as far as Hegel is concerned. It now remains to look at the final stage in this process of internalization by means of which the conditions of intuition are fully overcome: the 'absolute knowing' of philosophy.

CHAPTER 4

PHILOSOPHY: THE METAPHYSICS OF FREEDOM

1. LOGIC OR SPECULATIVE PHILOSOPHY

In addition to the philosophies of nature and spirit, Hegel's philosophical system contains another part concerned with that which he calls '*Logic* or *speculative philosophy*'.[1] Philosophy forms the highest moment of absolute spirit because it comprehends the content of both art and the revealed religion in purely conceptual terms, and is thus able to demonstrate that their content is essentially the same as its content. Yet, unlike these earlier forms of absolute spirit, logic or speculative philosophy constitutes a form of knowledge in which thought is both the form and content of knowledge, so that nothing remains alien to thought. This identity of form and content is the result of overcoming the conditions of intuition. In the *Phenomenology of Spirit*, this result is achieved through the gradual transition from a sensory form of consciousness, in which consciousness and its object are taken to be independent of each other, to pure knowing, in which thought is both the subject and the object of knowledge. Whereas in the *Encyclopaedia* there is a gradual transition from nature to absolute spirit, with the attempt to portray the divine in sensory form (i.e. art) being replaced by religious representational thought, whose content is in turn comprehended by philosophy in purely conceptual terms.

We saw in the previous chapter that the revealed religion, which forms the highest stage of absolute spirit next to philosophy, suffers from certain limitations with respect to its form (i.e. representational thought). These limitations all relate to a failure on the part of the revealed religion to transcend the conditions of intuition, since it employs images drawn from the sensible world, such as the image of Jesus as a person who once existed at a specific point in time and in a specific place. This in turn means that although the revealed religion's representations of the content that it shares in common with philosophy belong to the inner realm of representational thought, they still have a sensuous character. For Hegel, the defining feature of the sensory is singularity, since the items of intuition are mutually external to each other in virtue of the different points in space and time that they occupy. These items of intuition, when taken by themselves, do not, therefore, appear to stand in a necessary relation to each other, but are instead merely juxtaposed and appear to succeed each other in a random order; they therefore achieve order and unity only through being representations that belong to a single consciousness.[2] While the determinations of religious representational thought are thus linked together in an external fashion, in the case of Hegel's *Logic* the necessary relations existing between the various determinations of pure thought are allegedly demonstrated by means of the dialectical development through which they are generated. Consequently, Hegel thinks that he is able to show that the determinations in question are not simply juxtaposed and do not succeed each other in a merely random order.

Hegel's understanding of the essential differences between the pure thought of philosophy and other forms of knowledge, such as religious representational thought, will be seen to suggest a number of ways in which his *Logic* relates to the concept of freedom. Hegel himself suggests that a link between logic and the concept of freedom is demanded by the spirit of the times when he makes the following statement: 'The complete transformation which philosophical thought in Germany has undergone in the last twenty-five years and the higher standpoint reached by spirit in its awareness of itself, have had but little influence as yet on the structure of logic.'[3] This statement invites the question as to the precise nature of the transformation that has so far failed to have any influence on the structure of logic.

The transformation in question can be identified with the importance that Kant accords the idea of autonomy, which involves a refusal to grant validity to that which remains external to reason in the sense that it is impossible to have rational insight into it. This identification of the transformation that has so far failed to have any influence on the structure of logic with the idea of autonomy is suggested by Hegel's claim that, 'From now on the principle of the *independence of reason*, of its absolute inward autonomy, has to be regarded as the universal principle of philosophy, and as one of the assumptions of our times'.[4] Yet in spite of the transformation that Kant thus brought about in philosophical thought, Hegel thinks that Kant himself failed to incorporate the principle of autonomy into logic. By looking at Hegel's criticisms of what he calls subjective idealism, which he associates with both Kant and Fichte, we can gain a better understanding as to why he claims that there has been a failure to incorporate the principle of autonomy into the domain of logic.

We saw in Chapter 1 that Kant speaks of concepts or categories as forming the conditions of experience, in the sense that they perform a synthesizing function that makes a single organized experience possible. Experience also requires, however, a sensory content upon which the categories perform their synthesizing function by organizing and uniting representations into a single organized experience, as is required by the unity of apperception, that is, the necessity of thinking of all representations as being one and all my representations. As we have seen, the representations in question can, for Kant, only be given through the pure forms of intuition (i.e. space and time).

Kant thinks that one implication of his account of the conditions of the possibility of experience is that we can know objects only as they appear to us but not as they are in themselves. This is because our knowledge of objects is conditioned by the categories and the pure forms of intuition which first make a single organized experience possible for us; yet we cannot be sure that these conditions of our knowledge of objects equally apply to the objects themselves, that is, how they are independently of our cognitive relation to them. While it is not the case that Kant adopts an idealist position of the type that denies that things have any reality whatsoever except in so far as we perceive them, he does appear to deny that our representations of things correspond to how these things are independently of our way of knowing them, even though he does not deny the existence of these things, as he himself makes clear.[5]

Kant thus introduces a type of object whose essential nature cannot be known. The object in question can therefore be characterized only in purely negative terms as that which we cannot know but must nevertheless presuppose as a condition of experience.

Kant's thing-in-itself, like Fichte's not-'I', in this way remains external to the knowing subject, who cannot step outside the bounds of experience, in the sense that it forms a presupposition of experience into which we can gain no further insight other than the fact that it exists. Hegel thinks that this limitation to our knowledge is incompatible with the idea of the autonomy of reason, which demands that nothing should remain external to reason. Consequently, in the following passage he argues that although both Kant and Fichte accord the knowing subject an important role in determining the object of knowledge, the latter nevertheless retains its independence in the face of the knowing subject:

> True, in these systems, the thing-in-itself or the infinite shock or resistance principle [*Anstoss*] enters directly into the 'I' and becomes only something *for it*; but it proceeds from a free otherness which is perpetuated as a negative being-in-itself. The 'I' is therefore undoubtedly determined as ideal [*das Ideelle*], as being for itself, as infinite self-relation; but the moment of *being-for-one* is not completed to the point where the beyond, or the direction to the beyond, vanishes.[6]

The absolute independence that the object retains in its relation to the knowing subject leads Hegel to claim that Kant and Fichte fail to go beyond the standpoint of consciousness, which involves a type of relation in which the object remains external to the subject who is conscious of it.[7] This view of the matter may seem unfair in Fichte's case because of the debt that Hegel clearly owes him in relation to his own theory of the universal self-consciousness of spirit, in which each person recognizes him- or herself in others, so that the otherness of the object of consciousness is overcome. Nevertheless, even in the case of this universal self-consciousness, each person remains independent in relation to others not only in virtue of his or her capacity to be self-determining, but also in virtue of the fact that he or she exists as a physical object located at a determinate point in space and time.

Hegel's speculative logic, by contrast, presupposes that liberation from the opposition of consciousness has already been achieved.[8] For Hegel, speculative logic is for this reason not tied to the conditions of intuition, thus allowing thought to be its own object. This identity of the subject and object of thought means that we no longer need to presuppose the existence of an object such as the thing-in-itself or the not-'I' that remains independent of the relation of the knowing subject to its object. Moreover, Hegel himself considers the identity of the subject and object of thought attained in his speculative logic to be a form of freedom, as is evident from the following passage:

> But thinking is at home with itself, it relates itself to itself, and is its own ob-ject. Insofar as my ob-ject is a thought, I am at home with myself. Thus the I, or thinking, is infinite because it is related in thinking to an ob-ject that is itself. An ob-ject as such is an other, something negative that confronts me. But if thinking thinks itself, then it has an ob-ject that is at the same time not an ob-ject, i.e., an ob-ject that is sublated, ideal. Thus thinking as such, thinking in its purity, does not have any restriction within itself.[9]

In this passage, Hegel stresses an important aspect of his idea of freedom: the notion of being at home with oneself in one's other in the sense that one is able to identify oneself with one's object, so that the latter loses its appearance of otherness. The being at home with oneself in one's other is here absolute because the object (i.e. the content of thought) is no longer external to the thinking subject but is instead immanent to thought.

This brings me to the content of Hegel's *Logic*. As we shall see, Hegel understands this content to be one that is self-generated, and this marks another significant difference between him and Kant. Hegel is in fact highly critical of Kant's attempt to identify the categories by deriving them from the various types of judgement identified by traditional logic, whereas he thinks that Fichte's philosophy shows that the essential determinations of thought ought to be exhibited in their necessity by deducing them from thinking itself.[10] Hegel here has in mind Kant's claim that there must be the same number of pure concepts of the understanding as there are logical functions of judgement, because in both cases the act of bringing representations into unity is involved, so that the only use that the understanding makes of concepts is to judge by means of them.[11]

While Kant fails to offer a proper deduction of the pure forms of thought because he derives them from a body of knowledge (i.e. traditional logic) whose validity he simply accepts as something given, Fichte attempts to deduce the various concepts that make up what he calls the system of experience, which consists of the various laws of the intellect that need to be demonstrated in order to explain the feeling of necessity which accompanies specific representations.[12] However, the not-'I' remains essential to Fichte's attempt to deduce the system of experience, since it provides the empirical content which is organized according to the necessary laws of the 'I'. Consequently, although Hegel prefers Fichte's attempt to deduce the pure forms of thought to Kant's derivation of them from the various types of judgment identified by traditional logic, he cannot accept the way in which Fichte's deduction relies on the idea of something that is held to transcend thought.

Having established the identity of thought and its object, Hegel thinks that he is in a better position to deduce the pure determinations of thought in way that not only demonstrates their necessity but also treats them as the essential forms of reality; and we shall later see in more detail how Hegel takes the essential nature of our thought and the essential nature of reality to be the same. The fact that Hegel holds this view explains why he claims that the metaphysics which preceded Kant's critical philosophy stood at a higher level than the latter because it regarded the essential determinations of thought as constituting the fundamental determinations of things, and thus believed that 'the cognition of things as they are *in-themselves* results from the *thinking* of what *is*'.[13] Hegel therefore maintains that '*logic* coincides with *metaphysics*, with the science of *things* grasped in *thoughts* that used to be taken to express the *essentialities* of the *things*'.[14]

Hegel is, however, also critical of this pre-Kantian form of metaphysics because it understood thought to express the essence of things only, and thereby failed to comprehend the concept of subjectivity, which is an integral feature of both Kant's and Fichte's subjective idealism. For Hegel, this constitutes a failure on the part of the older metaphysics because 'everything turns on grasping and expressing the True, not only as *Substance*, but equally as *Subject*'.[15] He himself claims in fact that 'the living Substance is being which is in truth *Subject*, or, what is the same, is in truth actual only in so far as it is the movement of positing itself, or is the mediation of its self-othering with itself'.[16] In other words, the object of thought (i.e. substance) exhibits the freedom of being with itself in its other; and we shall see that the object of thought comes to exhibit this type of freedom when it is comprehended as that which Hegel calls the Idea.

The older form of metaphysics also lacked the right method for identifying the pure forms of thought, which culminate in a determination of thought that exhibits the freedom of being with one's self in one's other, and failed to offer a proper deduction of them. This brings me to Hegel's dialectical method, which I believe can be more fully understood by comparing it to the kind of 'external' thinking that he rejects on the grounds that it cannot provide an adequate knowledge of reality as it is in itself, and thus fails to comprehend and express the true not only as substance but also as subject. Since Hegel thinks that we find both the theory of the absolute as substance and an example of external thinking combined in the philosophy of Spinoza, I shall now turn to his critique of this particular example of pre-Kantian metaphysics before going on to describe his own dialectical method.

2. HEGEL'S CRITIQUE OF SPINOZA'S THEORY OF SUBSTANCE

In the *Science of Logic*, Hegel claims that the system of Spinoza is the philosophy which adopts the standpoint of substance and stops there.[17] He also states that Spinoza's concept of substance corresponds to the concept of the Absolute as presented in the section entitled the Absolute in the Doctrine of Essence, which forms the second book of his *Logic*.[18] Since the Doctrine of Essence is followed by the Doctrine of the Concept, we must assume that Spinoza's theory of substance represents an inadequate account of the Absolute, the true nature of which becomes explicit only at a later stage in the *Logic*. This would accord with the demand mentioned earlier to grasp and express the true not only as substance but also as subject; a demand which, as we shall see, Hegel attempts to satisfy in the Doctrine of the Concept. An important sense in which Spinoza's theory of substance represents an inadequate conception of the Absolute must therefore be seen as the way in which it comprehends the Absolute only as substance, that is, as the object of thought, but not also as subject.

Hegel also thinks that Spinoza fails to adopt the right kind of philosophical method which would have allowed him to comprehend the Absolute not only as substance but also as subject; for the method he employs fails to exhibit the necessity of the various determinations of substance, with the result that Spinoza is not able to go beyond the concept of substance, which he in any case simply presupposes. It should be noted, however, that Hegel does not understand his critique of Spinoza's theory of substance to be a purely negative enterprise; he in fact cites his account of Spinoza's system as the paradigm of what it means to refute a philosophical system. Such a refutation does not involve showing that a philosophical system is totally false; it instead involves understanding how this system is a necessary standpoint assumed by the Absolute, by which Hegel means a standpoint which speculative thought necessarily finds itself occupying in the course of the history of philosophy.[19] The task of the philosophical system which refutes an earlier one is therefore to recognize the standpoint of the latter as an essential and necessary one, even though it must take the further step of allowing this earlier system to raise itself to the higher standpoint of a genuinely speculative philosophy.[20] This implies that while Spinoza's theory of substance represents an inadequate account of the Absolute, it still contains an insight into its essential nature, albeit only a partial one. I shall now look at some criticisms that Hegel makes of Spinoza's theory of substance, in order to show why the latter represents an inadequate account of the Absolute, and then go on to identify the insight into the essential nature of the Absolute that is nevertheless contained in this theory.

For Hegel, one of the main defects of Spinoza's theory of substance concerns the way in which Spinoza identifies the various determinations of substance (i.e. its attributes and modes) by means of an act of *'external thinking'*.[21] An act of external thinking is one in which given determinations are applied or attributed to a given substrate, which is merely presupposed. The determinations in question are applied externally to this given substrate in the sense that they are not shown to result from the latter. This type of external thinking is for Hegel typical of pre-Kantian metaphysics in general, which simply attaches predicates to a given substrate, such as God or the soul, without investigating the validity of the determinations themselves, nor the procedure of attaching predicates to that which serves as their substrate.[22]

In the case of Spinoza's theory of substance, it is the concept of substance itself which serves as the substrate to which various determinations are then applied. Spinoza presupposes the concept of substance because he merely offers the following definition of it: 'By substance I understand what is in itself and is conceived through itself, that is, that whose concept does not require the concept of another thing, from which it must be formed'.[23] Since Spinoza equates causes with reasons,[24] this definition of substance as that which is in itself and conceived through itself can be taken to imply some kind of causal independence, whereby the existence or nature of one thing, in this case substance, does not need to be explained in terms of the existence or nature of another thing. For example, substance cannot be explained in terms of the existence of something that remains independent of it and which could have caused it to come into being or prevented it from existing. Spinoza fails to demonstrate why the concept of substance must be defined in this way, however.

An example of an act of external thinking, in which predicates are attached to a given substrate, is to be found in Spinoza's description of an attribute of substance as that which the intellect perceives of substance as constituting its essence.[25] For Spinoza, the human mind can identify two attributes of substance: thought and extension. Hegel thinks that Spinoza is unable to demonstrate the necessity of the attributes of thought and extension, however; and this is why he accuses Spinoza of taking up the attributes of substance as merely given determinations that are adopted empirically.[26]

One reason that Hegel has for claiming that Spinoza fails to demonstrate the necessity of the attributes of substance is that he provides the definition of an attribute of substance as that which the intellect perceives of substance as constituting its essence before he has given an account of the human intellect, which he characterizes as a mode of thinking.[27] For Spinoza defines a mode as an affection of substance; a mode cannot therefore be conceived through itself alone, but instead requires the concept of another thing (i.e. the concept of substance and at least one of its attributes, in this case thought) through which it must be conceived.[28] By contrast, an attribute of substance is substance, although substance as it is perceived by the intellect in a certain way. This means that an attribute will share the essential nature of substance, including the fact that it must be conceived through itself and is therefore a concept that does not require the concept of another thing from which it must be formed. As previously mentioned, the fact that Spinoza equates causes with reasons suggests that his description of substance as that which is conceived through itself implies some kind of causal independence, whereby the existence or nature of one thing does not need to be explained in terms of the existence or nature of another thing. All singular human thoughts or feelings of one's own body and its affections, on the other hand, as modes of substance, cannot be regarded as self-subsistent entities, since they can only be fully explained with reference to at least one of the attributes of substance (i.e. thought or extension) and to substance itself.

The way in which Spinoza distinguishes between the modes and attributes of substance raises a problem with regard to his definition of an attribute as that which the intellect perceives of substance as constituting its essence. For while an attribute of substance is, like substance itself, held by Spinoza to be ontologically prior to a mode of substance, he appears to presuppose the existence of the individual intellect, which is a mode of substance, so as to explain how it is possible to identify the attributes of substance, even though the attribute of thought is meant to be ontologically prior to its modes. In other words, this attribute of substance can be explained only with reference to something other than itself (i.e. the individual intellect). In short, although the individual intellect, as a mode of substance, is supposed to be conceived through the attribute of thought, things now appear to be the other way round, with a mode of substance having to be invoked in order to explain an attribute of substance. This inversion of the ontological order which is held by Spinoza to characterize the relation of the modes of substance to the attributes of substance may be taken as evidence of a failure on his part to exhibit the necessity with which these determinations proceed from the concept of substance; for a necessary process, through which the concept of substance, then the attributes of thought and extension, and finally the modes of substance are generated, appears to be lacking.

Another reason Hegel has for claiming that Spinoza's theory of substance involves an act of external thinking is due to another feature of his account of the attributes of substance. As I have already mentioned, an attribute of substance is substance, although substance as it is perceived by the intellect in a certain way. This implies that an attribute will share the essential nature of substance, which must be thought to include its being a concept which does not require the concept of another thing from which it must be formed, so that it can be conceived through itself alone. There is, however, one sense in which Spinoza would have to concede that the attributes of substance must themselves be conceived through something else and in this respect cannot be said to share the essential nature of substance. This is because the concept of substance must be thought to be ontologically prior to its attributes, since it is only possible to speak of thought and extension as attributes of a single substance if one already presupposes the concept of a single substance; for otherwise there appears to be no reason why the attributes cannot themselves be called substances, as happens in Descartes' account of thought and extension as two distinct substances. Moreover, the attributes of thought and extension can each be negatively defined as that which the other is not, so that once again we appear to have something that must be conceived through something else. The way in which an attribute of substance is a concept which appears to require the concept of another thing (i.e. substance and another attribute) from which it must be formed serves to undermine the distinction which Spinoza makes between an attribute and a mode of substance; for he defines a mode of substance as that which cannot be conceived through itself alone, and thus requires the concept of another thing from which it must be formed. Yet this definition can now be seen to apply equally to the attributes of substance.

This view of the matter helps to explain why Hegel claims that although the attribute is supposed to be understood from itself alone, it contains otherness and cannot be understood from itself alone, so that it is only in the mode of the Absolute that the determination of the attribute is really posited.[29] This reduction of the attributes of the Absolute to modes of the Absolute also finds expression in Hegel's claim that 'the totality is posited as Absolute, or the attribute has the absolute for its content and subsistence; its form determination, by virtue of which it is attribute, is therefore also posited, immediately as mere illusory being – the negative as a negative'.[30] The idea here appears to be that the attribute of the Absolute is merely an expression of the Absolute rather than a self-subsistent entity, and as such it must be thought to lack any genuine independence, just as Spinoza must himself allow. The attribute of the Absolute is thus reduced to the same status as the mode of the Absolute; and this reduction of each and every determination of the Absolute to a mode of the latter leads Hegel to claim that Spinoza's substance is only 'the universal might of negation . . . the dark, shapeless abyss . . . in which all determinate content is swallowed up as radically null and void, and which produces nothing out of itself that has a positive subsistence of its own'.[31]

Spinoza's apparent failure to show how the intellect and attributes of substance derive from the concept of substance in the very same order in which he himself places them, along with his failure to maintain a firm distinction between the attributes and modes of substance, lend support to two of Hegel's main criticisms of his theory of substance: the criticism that Spinoza fails to provide a convincing account of the various essential determinations of substance which provide the latter with determinacy, and the criticism that the determinations of substance are 'only enumerated *one after the other*, without any inner sequence of development'.[32] For Hegel, these criticisms are linked to Spinoza's method, which involves setting up various definitions and axioms whose truth is merely presupposed, and from which he then attempts to derive a series of theorems *ordine geometrico*. As well as resting on certain presuppositions, this method is not, for Hegel, one in which form and content exhibit the kind of absolute unity that is required to exhibit the necessity of the determinations of pure thought which constitute the essential nature of reality as it is in itself. Hegel's dialectical method, by contrast, is held by him to exhibit an absolute unity of form and content which allows the determinations of pure thought to emerge out of each other. Moreover, he does not consider the starting point of his *Logic* to be question-begging, unlike Spinoza's theory of the Absolute as substance, which rests on a definition whose validity has not itself been demonstrated.

In spite of the various criticisms that Hegel makes of Spinoza's theory of substance, Spinoza can be credited with comprehending the Absolute as an unconditioned totality, even though he fails to demonstrate the necessity of its determinations and to make this unconditioned totality into something more than an abstraction. As we shall see, Hegel's account of the absolute Idea is also meant to provide an account of an unconditioned totality, though this time one in which the Absolute is grasped and expressed not only as substance but also as subject. First, however, we need to consider Hegel's method in more detail, since it is by means of the latter that he seeks to demonstrate the necessity of comprehending and expressing the Absolute as the Idea.

From Hegel's criticisms of Spinoza's method we can already identify the demands that this method will need to meet: 1) the demand not to presuppose a given substrate in the way that Spinoza does when he introduces the concept of substance in the form of a definition; 2) the demand to deduce the various thought-determinations that provide the Absolute with determinacy in a way that demonstrates the necessity of the logical order in which they emerge; and 3) the demand for unity of form and content, so as to avoid an 'external' type of thinking. This last demand has to some extent already been met because Hegel thinks that thought has itself as its object at the level of logic or speculative philosophy. Nevertheless, as we shall see, he also seeks to demonstrate this unity of form (i.e. thought) and content (i.e. that which is thought) within the realm of pure thought itself.

3. HEGEL'S DIALECTICAL METHOD

Hegel describes the logical as such, with regard to its form, as having three sides: the side of abstraction or of the understanding, the dialectical or negatively rational side, and the speculative or positively rational side.[33] We must therefore assume that these three sides of the logical have a role to play in the development that the object of thought undergoes in his *Logic*, which employs a method that is not externally applied to a given content but instead shows itself to be immanent to its content. Since Hegel's account of the concept of being, with which his *Logic* begins, not only exhibits all three sides of the logical with regard to its form, but also involves an attempt on Hegel's part to avoid presupposing a given substrate, it exemplifies both his understanding of the logical as such and his dialectical method, which he opposes to any kind of 'external' thinking.

Hegel begins his *Logic* with the concept of being because at this stage we have only the idea of thought thinking itself, an idea which has shown itself to be the result of the process through which the opposition of consciousness is overcome. While Hegel's account of how the opposition between consciousness and its object is overcome, as given in the *Phenomenology of Spirit* and his *Encyclopaedia* philosophy of spirit, is meant to justify the standpoint of pure knowing, which would otherwise constitute a presupposition into which we have no real insight, this form of knowledge still lacks a determinate content of its own. Consequently, at the very beginning of the *Logic*, the object of pure thought must be that which is completely empty and indeterminate; and Hegel thinks that this absolute emptiness and indeterminacy finds expression in the concept of pure being.

The necessity of beginning with the empty and indeterminate thought of pure being represents Hegel's attempt to avoid introducing a given substrate which is merely presupposed. We shall see, moreover, that Hegel thinks that more determinate thoughts than that of pure being involve a process of mediation, since they are what they are only in relation to other thought-determinations. Any attempt to introduce a more determinate thought at the beginning of the *Logic* would therefore involve presupposing other thoughts whose necessity had not been demonstrated. In other words, the first determination of thought of the *Logic* must be immediate in the sense that it does not need to be explained in terms of other thoughts; and, given its complete lack of determinacy, the concept of pure being is held by Hegel to meet this requirement. On the other hand, the concept of being is the result of the process in which the opposition of consciousness is overcome, and in this respect it is the result of mediation.

The beginning of the *Logic* thus expresses nothing more than the idea of the identity of thought and its object, which finds expression in the concept of being. Yet this concept is so indeterminate that it lacks any form of inward or outward distinction. In other words, it lacks any distinctive features that might serve to distinguish it from other objects of thought with which it might stand in some kind of relation. As Hegel himself puts it, pure being is 'equal only to itself. It is also not unequal relatively to an other; it has no diversity within itself nor any with a reference outwards'.[34] Yet such indeterminacy and emptiness is, Hegel claims, equally expressed by the concept of nothing, which is also 'simply equality with itself, complete emptiness, absence of all determination and content'.[35] Being and nothing thus turn out to be identical.

In order to understand what Hegel means by this identity of being and nothing, it may help to recall his criticisms of Jacobi's identification of God with the words 'it is'; for this invites a comparison with Hegel's account of pure being, which is immediate or unmediated, in the sense that it involves mere self-identity and does not exhibit any internal features that might serve to distinguish it from the concept of nothing. As we have seen, Hegel's main criticism of Jacobi's conception of God is that, by identifying God with the statement 'it is', Jacobi asserts only that God exists and thus fails to specify what God is. In short, as Hegel's description of the thought of pure being makes clear, the words 'it is' cannot be said to provide a determinate representation of God. Hegel in fact pursues the analogy between an abstract conception of God and the concept of being, which he takes to imply the concept of nothing, when he states that the idea of God as the supreme essence is the same abstraction as the nothing which the Buddhists make into the principle of everything.[36]

If we now return to the three sides of the logical as such that Hegel identifies, we can see that the first of them, the side of the abstraction or of the understanding, appears to give rise to a contradiction in the case of the concepts of being and nothing. For Hegel, the understanding, which belongs to the realm of representational thought, 'stops short at the fixed determinacy and its distinctness vis-à-vis other determinacies'.[37] In other words, the understanding views thoughts in isolation from each other, and it therefore treats thoughts that appear to be opposed to each other as being mutually exclusive. In the present case, the understanding holds that the concepts of being and nothing express entirely different thoughts which are completely opposed to each other, so that they cannot be held to be the same. Hegel, however, believes that he has shown how the concepts of being and nothing must be considered as qualitatively indistinguishable from each other. The understanding is thus faced with the contradiction that, on the one hand, the concepts of being and nothing are held to be completely different from, and opposed to, each other; yet, on the other hand, these concepts have been shown to be essentially the same and therefore not different from, and opposed to, each other. According to Hegel, this contradiction even finds expression in the proposition that being and nothing are the same: for while this proposition asserts the identity of these concepts, they in fact appear as two distinct concepts within this proposition, which thus also distinguishes them from each other, with the result that 'the proposition is self-contradictory and cancels itself out'.[38]

The contradiction which now confronts the understanding constitutes the dialectical or negatively rational side of the logical as such, which has shown itself to be the result of the understanding's own attempt to treat the concepts of being and nothing as isolated determinations of thought. The result is a negative one because it looks as if we must simply reject the understanding's attempt to treat the thoughts of being and nothing as distinct from each other, or else reject Hegel's claim that the concept of being shows itself to be qualitatively the same as the concept of nothing. While Hegel would obviously reject the second approach, the first one is for him an unsatisfactory one because collapsing the distinction between being and nothing would result in a return to the point at which we began, namely the indeterminate and empty self-identity of being, though this time it would be a matter of indifference whether we called it being or nothing. Consequently, Hegel wants to preserve the distinction between being and nothing that the understanding makes, even though he remains equally committed to the dialectical or negatively rational moment to which the identity of being and nothing gives rise.

Hegel's attempt to preserve the distinction between being and nothing is to be found in his account of the concept of becoming, which, when analysed, turns out to contain within itself both being and nothing, either as coming-to-be, in which case thought moves from nothing to being, or as ceasing-to-be, in which case thought moves from being to nothing. In other words, the concept of becoming expresses the way in which an analysis of the concept of being forces the understanding to identify the latter with the concept of nothing and is then, in a vain attempt to maintain an absolute distinction between these two concepts, made to move helplessly from one thought to the other, so that being 'becomes' nothing and nothing 'becomes' being. Yet this process has a positive result which the understanding fails to recognize; for the concept of becoming allows us to maintain both the identity and difference of the concepts of being and nothing. This is because they are, on the one hand, unified in the concept of becoming, in which they are reduced to moments, while, on the other hand, as moments of becoming, they are distinct from each other, even if they no longer possess the kind of self-subsistence that the understanding attributes to them. As Hegel himself puts it, 'being and nothing are distinct moments; becoming only *is*, in so far as they are distinguished. This third is an other than they; they subsist only in an other, which is equivalent to saying that they are not self-subsistent'.[39]

Hegel thinks that he is thus able to preserve the distinction between being and nothing within a new concept, becoming. Since this new determination of thought contains both being and nothing within itself, it is more concrete than these earlier abstract thoughts, which turn out to be qualitatively indistinguishable from each other. This opposition within unity constitutes the speculative or positively rational side of the logical as such; and Hegel therefore describes speculative thought as the grasping of opposites in their unity.[40] The result is here a positive one because it contains the two other sides of the logical as such, the side of abstraction or of the understanding and the dialectical or negatively rational side, within itself.

The way in which being and nothing are preserved as moments of becoming, together with the way in which the two other sides of the logical as such are preserved in the speculative side, serve to illustrate one of Hegel's key terms for which there is no single word in English that captures all its senses: the German word *aufheben*, which is often translated as 'sublate'. This term can mean both to preserve or maintain and to cease or put an end to, and it therefore has two apparently contrary meanings. Hegel considers this to be an example of how a speculative meaning can be found in everyday language.[41] He also compares the double meaning of the German word *aufheben* favourably with the meaning of the Latin word *tollere* when he claims that the affirmative determination of the latter signifies only a raising or lifting up, whereas something is *aufgehoben* only in so far as it has entered into unity with its opposite. In the case of being and nothing, we might say that they are preserved as moments of the more determinate concept of becoming, thus losing their immediacy or one-sidedness, in the sense that they are no longer treated as isolated self-subsistent thoughts. The same could be said of the side of abstraction or of the understanding and the dialectical or negatively rational side of the logical as such, which are both preserved as moments of the speculative or positively rational side.

Although becoming represents for Hegel a more adequate and deeper knowledge of being and nothing, this does not mean that these concepts no longer have a significant role to play in his *Logic*. Hegel in fact views the unity of being and nothing (or non-being) as the ground of all the further determinations of thought found in the *Logic*, though this is not to say that they possess the same meaning as they possess at the beginning of the latter. We here encounter another way in which being and nothing are preserved; and the way in which they are thus preserved in later parts of the *Logic* is nowhere more evident than in Hegel's account of the thought-determination that he calls 'determinate being' or 'being-there' (*Dasein*), which succeeds becoming as the object of pure thought.

By looking at Hegel's account of determinate being or being-there, we shall, moreover, encounter another distinctive feature of his thought, his understanding of true infinity.

The concept of becoming is inherently unstable because it involves a constant logical movement from being to nothing and from nothing to being. Being-there or determinate being is, by contrast, a more stable unity of being and nothing (or non-being) because being here has the shape of reality, by which Hegel means the identity of the being of something with the essential quality that makes this something into what it is. In spite of this identification of something with what positively distinguishes it from something else, reality nevertheless implies non-being in the form of negation, since we can understand what something is only by also knowing what it is not.

A good example of what Hegel means by this is to be found in the case of different colours. In his account of the thought-determination 'thing', which is given in the second book of the *Logic*, the Doctrine of Essence, Hegel claims that having replaces being.[42] This is because a thing is understood to have various properties from which it itself remains distinct, in the sense that, as the bearer of such properties, it cannot be viewed as identical with its properties, even when they are taken together as a whole. Hegel's account of determinate being, by contrast, belongs to the first book of the *Logic*, the Doctrine of Being, in which having is yet to replace being. The determination of thought which he terms something is therefore, unlike the thing with properties, immediately one with its quality, so that if it lost this quality, it would cease to be the something that it is. Colours in this respect provide an especially good example of such a 'something' because they are themselves properties, as opposed to being bearers of them. In short, each colour is what it is in virtue of the fact that it is qualitatively distinct from other colours which are also identical with their particular quality.

If we use colours as an example of how our understanding of something depends on what the latter is not, Hegel can be seen to have in mind the idea that it is impossible to regard particular colours as standing in complete isolation from each other; for each particular colour is what it is in virtue of its being distinct from other colours; so that our understanding of the colour red, for example, involves our contrasting it with other colours. In other words, understanding what the colour red is will also involve knowing that it is not blue, not green, not yellow, and so on. Hegel takes this to mean that each determinate being must be thought to exclude or negate, as he puts it, other determinate beings. Consequently, that which each determinate being is not, or its negation, must be held to constitute a condition of our being able to identify something as the determinate being that it is.

Reality and negation are therefore seen by Hegel to be essential moments of determinate being, so that we once again have a speculative thought in which two distinct determinations of thought, which the understanding seeks to hold apart, are grasped as moments of a higher unity. In the case of the concept of something, Hegel identifies these two thought-determinations as being-for-another and being-in-itself. Being-for-another concerns the way in which something must be understood in terms of that which it is not (e.g. not blue, not green, or not yellow), while being-in-itself concerns its own essential quality (e.g. redness). Since being-for-another is as essential as being-in-itself when it comes to understanding what something is, Hegel claims that 'otherness is not something indifferent outside it, but its own moment'.[43]

Hegel's understanding of something as the unity of being-in-itself and being-for-another leads him to speak of the negation of the negation. By this he means that while we have the negation of something by something else, since the latter has the appearance of a limit or restriction in relation to the former, the something, which thus appears to be limited by something else, is what it is because of this something else, in the sense that it can be fully understood only with reference to that with which it can be meaningfully contrasted, that is to say, with something of the same general type as itself. In other words, while something is limited by something else in the sense that the latter is not the former, the limit in question can nevertheless be understood as a type of self-limitation because this something else at the same time forms an essential moment of the something, in the sense that our understanding of the latter implies the former. This in turn means that while the first negation is to be understood as the limitation of something by something else, and thus appears to involve a purely negative type of relation, the second negation concerns the way in which something has the first negation as a moment of its own self, since its relation to this something else is equally a condition of its being what it is.

The idea of the negation of the negation brings me to the account of infinity that Hegel gives in the section on determinate being.

According to Hegel, at the name of the infinite 'the heart and the mind light up, for in the infinite the spirit is not merely abstractly present to itself, but rises to its own self, to the light of its thinking, of its universality, of its freedom'.[44] The fact that Hegel here associates the infinite with freedom is, as I hope to show, highly significant in relation to the highest thought-determination of his *Logic*, the absolute Idea; for I shall suggest that in the case of the latter two projects coincide: the project of fully incorporating the principle of autonomy into the domain of logic and the project of treating the content of logic as 'the exposition of God as he is in his eternal essence before the creation of nature and a finite spirit'.[45]

With respect to the second of these projects, Hegel appears to suggest that we should read his *Logic* as some kind of metaphysical theology, in which infinity, which has traditionally been considered to be one of the attributes of God, is shown, through a dialectical process, to be an essential feature of the Absolute, rather than its being treated as a predicate that is to be applied to a representation of God which serves as the kind of substrate found in pre-Kantian metaphysics. This impression is strengthened by Hegel's claim that since the only object of philosophy is God, 'philosophy *is* theology, and [one's] occupation with philosophy – or rather *in* philosophy – is of itself the service of God'.[46] Moreover, he goes on to describe the object of philosophy as that which is 'strictly in and for itself *the unconditioned*, the free, the unbounded, that which is its own purpose and ultimate goal'.[47] We shall later see how this description of the object of philosophy as the unconditioned accords with Hegel's account of the absolute Idea.

Hegel defines the infinite as 'the negation of the negation, affirmation, *being* which has restored itself out of limitedness'.[48] He makes a distinction, however, between two types of infinite: the spurious or finitized infinite of the understanding and the genuine infinite of reason. As we might expect from the way in which Hegel associates the spurious infinite with the understanding, this type of infinity involves a conception of the infinite that holds the latter to be qualitatively distinct from, and opposed to, the finite. In other words, the infinite and the finite are both viewed as determinate beings each standing in isolation from the other. However, as is the case with determinate being in general, the infinite and the finite cannot be properly understood without reference to each other, since, 'In *saying* what the infinite is, namely the negation of the *finite*, the latter is itself included in what is *said*; it cannot be dispensed with for the definition or determination of the infinite'.[49] This appears to make the infinite into one particular thought next to another particular thought; and Hegel therefore argues that the infinite is turned into something finite because the finite, as the other of the infinite, limits and negates the latter. This gives rise to the contradiction that the infinite, which the understanding holds to be essentially different from the finite, turns out on closer inspection to be qualitatively the same as the finite, just as being and nothing turn out to be essentially the same. Consequently, the spurious infinite is held by Hegel to be an infinite progress consisting of an endless succession of finite items and a series whose completion remains a logical impossibility. In the case of determinate being, the spurious infinite arises because the concept of something implies the concept of an other or something else, which is itself just as much a something that implies the concept of an other which is also a something; so that, as Hegel himself puts it, 'Something becomes an other, but the other is itself a something, so it likewise becomes an other, and so on *ad infinitum*'.[50]

Rather than understanding the infinite and the finite to be simply qualitatively distinct from, and opposed to, each other, Hegel characteristically attempts to show how they are united in the concept of true infinity. He thinks, moreover, that the idea of the negation of the negation provides the type of infinity which avoids the kind of infinite progress mentioned above. As we have seen with the concept of something, the negation of the first negation, that is, the limitation to which something is subject through its relation to something else, can be viewed as a type of self-limitation because something is what it is through its not being something else. In this respect, something is both itself and an other (i.e. something else), and it thus returns to itself from this other in the sense that it has the latter as a moment of itself. This would also be true of the concepts of the infinite and finite in so far as they are understood as determinate beings. Consequently, Hegel does not identify true infinity with the non-finite; he instead identifies it with the whole movement exhibited by the negation of the negation, so that the true infinite must be thought to contain the finite as a moment of itself. Since this movement involves a return from the moment of otherness in the sense indicated above, he claims that 'the image of true infinity, bent back into itself, becomes the *circle*, the line which has reached itself, which is closed and wholly present, without *beginning* and *end*'.[51]

The idea of a return from otherness leads Hegel to claim that the genuine infinite consists in 'remaining at home with itself in its other, or (when it is expressed as a process) in coming to itself in its other'.[52] We have already witnessed the importance that the idea of remaining at home with oneself in one's other has for Hegel when we saw how the idea of thought thinking itself serves as a specific example of remaining at home with oneself in one's other, since form and content are here held to be the same. We might also add that by thinking dialectically, the thinking subject generates its own content, that is, the content of pure thought. Hegel therefore describes the Idea, which is the end result of this dialectical process, in terms that suggest an act of self-legislation, as 'the self-developing totality of its own peculiar determinations and laws, which thinking does not already *have* and find given within itself, but which it gives to itself'.[53] In addition to these different ways in which the *Logic* incorporates the principle of autonomy, the content of thought itself will now be seen to exhibit the character of that which remains at home with itself in its other, so that the thinking subject comes to have that which is truly infinite and unconditioned as its object. Hegel calls the object in question the absolute Idea.

4. THE IDEA

Hegel's *Logic* is divided into three main books: the Doctrine of Being, the Doctrine of Essence, and the Doctrine of the Concept. His account of the Idea belongs to the Doctrine of the Concept, which he distinguishes from the other two books of the *Logic* by calling it the subjective logic, whereas the Doctrine of Being and the Doctrine of Essence together form the objective logic. According to Hegel, the latter takes the place of the ontology of pre-Kantian metaphysics, which was supposed to investigate the nature of the *ens* (Latin: 'thing') in general.[54]

In Chapter 1 we saw that Fichte identifies the *ens* with the thing-in-itself which dogmatism takes to be independent of the self, to which it thus stands opposed, and which it determines, so that the self loses its freedom and independence. This suggests that we should think of the Doctrine of Being and the Doctrine of Essence as dealing with thoughts that apply to that which is taken to be independent of, and opposed to, the thinking self, that is to say, a thing-like entity which is viewed first as being and then as essence. Such an interpretation would accord with the fact that, as mentioned above, Hegel is critical of the pre-Kantian form of metaphysics because it understood thought to express the essence of things only; for this implies that this type of metaphysics failed to comprehend the concept of subjectivity, which is an integral feature of the subjective idealism of Kant and Fichte.

This interpretation is also suggested by the fact that, in the first part of the Doctrine of the Concept, Hegel turns to various forms of judgement and syllogism taken from traditional logic, though he seeks to demonstrate the necessity of these forms of thought by means of his dialectical method, rather than taking them from traditional logic, as he thinks Kant does; for this implies a transition in which the object of thought turns out to be the activity of thought itself. We would therefore seem to have a transition from determinations of thought that are, in the objective logic, taken to apply to a thing-like entity which is held to be independent of thought to determinations of thought that are, in the subjective logic, held to belong to thought as such.

The transition in question merely makes explicit what is already the case in the earlier books of the *Logic*, however: the fact that it is the dialectical activity of thought itself which generates the content of Hegel's *Logic*, so that thought, in so far as it proceeds dialectically, is not determined by anything external to it, and to which its activity must conform. In short, the transition from the objective to the subjective logic marks the point at which thought is fully recognized as being both the subject (i.e. that which thinks) and the object (i.e. that which is thought) of the *Logic*, even though this identity of the subject and object of thought is already implicitly present at the very beginning of the *Logic*, which presupposes that the opposition between subject and object that characterizes consciousness has been overcome. Consequently, the thinking self is now in the position to grasp its content as the product of its own activity, as opposed to taking its thinking activity to be determined by an object that remains independent of thought; and this is why Hegel understands the transition from the objective logic to the subjective logic as the transition from necessity to freedom.[55] The subjective logic thus involves an explicit awareness on the part of the thinking self of the autonomy of its own thought, in the sense that the thinking self obeys a law (i.e. the law of dialectical development through which its content is generated) that is equally the product of its own activity. The identity of the subject and object of thought which for Hegel becomes explicit in the subjective logic is, however, fully demonstrated only in the Idea, since in the case of the latter the object of thought itself exhibits the type of freedom that consists in being with oneself in one's other, with the result that the thinking self is able to achieve knowledge of its own essence, which is freedom.

For Hegel, the absolute Idea most fully exhibits the freedom of being with oneself in one's other because the identity of thought and its content is what defines it, in the sense that the essential structure of thought has been shown to be immanent to the object of thought. Hegel therefore describes the Idea as '*the absolute unity of Concept and objectivity*', so that its 'ideal content is nothing but the Concept in its determinations', while its 'real content is only the presentation that the Concept gives itself in the form of external thereness'.[56]

By the 'ideal content' of the Idea, Hegel means the three moments of the Concept (i.e. universality, particularity and individuality), whose necessity he thinks he has demonstrated in the first part of the Doctrine of the Concept. As previously mentioned, Hegel understands these three moments to be necessarily related to each other, rather than their being independent entities that can be fully understood in isolation from each other. By the 'real content', which constitutes the other aspect of the Idea, is meant the three moments of the Concept as instantiated in the object of thought. Since, for Hegel, the Idea is the truth, which he describes as the correspondence of objectivity with the Concept,[57] he holds something to be true only when it exhibits the three moments of the Concept in such a way that they can be grasped as the necessary moments of a single totality.

Given Hegel's description of it, the Idea can be regarded as absolute in the sense that, since it contains the object as one of its moments, the latter can no longer be regarded as independent of thought. Consequently, thought, as the Idea, is not determined by something that remains independent of it, such as a thing-in-itself or not-'I'. Thought thus realizes the model of true infinity that Hegel identifies earlier in the *Logic* with respect to both the form and the content of thought; for it is both itself and its other, that is, subject and object, in the sense that it negates the otherness of its other (i.e. objectivity) by making this other into a moment of itself. Since the Idea thus shows itself to be both infinite and unconditioned (i.e. not determined by something other than itself), the object of pure thought now exhibits these attributes which have traditionally been predicated of God. Moreover, since the absolute Idea, which forms the highest object of thought, exhibits the freedom of remaining with itself in its otherness, substance (i.e. the object) has been grasped as subject, that is, as that which is essentially self-determining.

In accordance with the aims and character of his dialectical method, Hegel seeks to demonstrate the necessity of thinking of the absolute Idea as the unity of subjectivity and objectivity. However, I shall here restrict myself to identifying what motivates Hegel's attempt to demonstrate the necessity of thinking of the absolute Idea in this way. To begin with, the wish to offer a philosophical reinterpretation of the God of traditional theism seems to have played a part, as we might have expected from Hegel's philosophy of religion, which I discussed in Chapter 3. Secondly, Hegel clearly wishes to show that we can reject the idea of an object that is independent of thought, an object that is still a feature of the subjective idealism of Kant and Fichte, who introduce the idea of the thing-in-itself and the not-'I' respectively. By so doing, Kant and Fichte invite the question as to whether we can really know what the thing-in-itself or the not-'I' essentially is. Kant himself acknowledges this problem when he claims that we can know only appearances and not things-in-themselves, and it is also suggested by the way in which Fichte is reduced to describing the not-'I' in purely negative terms. The independence of the object implies, in short, that it ultimately remains inaccessible to thought.

Hegel, by contrast, thinks that he has demonstrated that the essential determinations of thought (i.e. the moments of the Concept) are immanent to the object of thought, so that these determinations hold not only for the thinking self but also for the object of thought. In other words, Hegel thinks that he has demonstrated that thought is immanent to the object, which can therefore no longer be said to transcend thought. Although this demonstration takes place within the realm of pure thought, which suggests that the object in question is itself a determination of thought, rather than an object existing independently of thought in the external world, Hegel appears to think that his account of the Idea has implications for both the philosophies of nature and subjective spirit, in which the object is independent of thought in virtue of its presence in space and time. For he suggests that the identity of thought and its object that finds expression in the Idea enables the thinking self to know that there is no antithesis between its own thinking activity, whether it involves a purely theoretical attitude or an attempt to transform the world in accordance with its purposes, and the objective world.[58] In this respect, the ultimate aim of Hegel's *Logic* can be understood as the wish to demonstrate the identity of thought and being, thus allowing the thinking self, whether its activity is of a theoretical or practical kind, to remain at home with itself in its other, which this time has the shape of the object of its theoretical or practical concern.

CONCLUSION

We have seen that Hegel's idea of freedom has two main aspects: the negative freedom of the arbitrary will, which involves the freedom to choose but does not specify the content which the subject should make its own, and positive freedom, which finds expression in Kant's theory of moral autonomy. While negative freedom is assigned its rightful place in civil society in Hegel's philosophy of right, positive freedom is realized in a number of ways in Hegel's philosophical system: as objectified will in the case of right, so that the latter can be understood as an expression of the subjective will; as the essential relation between the subjective and objective moments of faith in the Christian religion; and as the idea of thought thinking itself and giving itself its own content in the *Logic*.

We also saw that the positive conception of freedom can be characterized as the notion of being at home with oneself in one's other, with the subject being able to identify itself with its object because the latter loses its appearance of otherness. In Hegel's *Logic*, the type of freedom in question assumes the form of the thinking subject's unity with its other (i.e. the object of its thought), in the sense that the conditions of intuition have allegedly been overcome at the level of 'absolute knowing', so that the object is no longer external to the thinking subject but is instead immanent to thought.

The description of freedom as being at home with oneself with one's other could be equally applied, however, to Hegel's theory of the universal self-consciousness of spirit, in which each self-consciousness recognizes itself in others while retaining its independence in relation to them. Yet the freedom of being at home with oneself with one's other here takes on a very different shape from the one that it assumes in Hegel's *Logic*. For while the latter involves an identity of the thinking self and its object which reaches the point of self-enclosedness, the fact that the conditions of intuition still apply in the case of finite spirit means that each self-consciousness encounters others who are externally present to it in space and time. Moreover, these others remain self-determining within the sphere left open to them through the act of self-limitation that each self-consciousness performs. In the universal self-consciousness of spirit, the other thus retains its otherness, even if this otherness is not absolute because of the equally essential moment of recognition.

The fact that freedom as being at home with oneself in one's other can be seen to assume different shapes depending on the context in which it is found suggests that the different parts of Hegel's system can be understood in relative independence of each other. On the other hand, Hegel thinks that these different shapes of positive freedom exhibit a similar structure; and, given the fact that the *Logic* is meant to provide an account of the basic determinations of reality in the most perspicuous form possible (i.e. a purely conceptual form of knowledge), we must assume that the structure of freedom understood as being at home with oneself in one's other is exhibited in this part of his system. Hegel's remarks on the relation of the *Logic* to the other parts of his system are ambiguous, however. For example, he describes the philosophies of nature and spirit as applied logic because the *Logic* is their animating soul, so that nature and spirit are 'only a particular mode of expression of the forms of pure thinking'.[1] While this implies that the essential determinations of nature and spirit can ultimately be expressed in terms of the determinations of pure thought, the situation begins to look less clear if we turn to a particular example of Hegel's attempt to apply logic to the other parts of his system.

The example in question concerns Hegel's philosophy of right. Hegel claims that the necessity of the development of the system of right is to be found in the '*immanent* progression and production of its own determinations', which is 'assumed to be familiar from logic'.[2] In other words, the determinations of his system of right arise through a dialectical process in the course of which one determination reveals itself to be inadequate in some way and thus gives rise to a higher determination in which this limitation is overcome. The fact that Hegel calls the process in question an immanent one suggests that the philosophy of right undergoes its own internal development in a way that accords with the dialectical method also found in his *Logic*; yet this does not imply that the development which the concept of right undergoes is based on Hegel's speculative logic.

With respect to the relation between his system of right and his *Logic*, Hegel states in the Preface to the *Elements of the Philosophy of Right* that although, on account of the concrete and inherently varied nature of the subject matter, he has omitted to demonstrate and bring out the logical progression in each and every detail, both the work as a whole and the construction of its parts are based on the 'logical spirit'. This statement again does not imply that the structure of Hegel's system of right is determined by the structure of the *Logic*, rather than its first undergoing its own internal development which can, on reflection, be seen to correspond to certain features of the *Logic*. Consequently, when Hegel claims that the constitution of the political state is rational in so far as it '*differentiates* and determines its activity within itself *in accordance with the nature of the concept*',[3] he can be thought to mean only that the political state shows itself to divide into three elements (i.e. the legislature, the executive and the constitutional monarchy) which can, on reflection, be seen to correspond to the three moments of the concept (i.e. universality, particularity and individuality).[4] We witnessed something similar in the case of the concept of the will; and one could therefore argue that although the phenomenon of the will, like that of the political state, shows itself to be explicable in terms of the moments of universality, particularity and individuality, this does not mean that Hegel is seeking to reduce all phenomena to the determinations of his *Logic*.

We may conclude, therefore, that Hegel himself thought that the different parts of his system could be understood in relative isolation from each other in spite of his view of philosophy and its object, the truth, as being essentially a system. In this respect, it appears that the various aspects of his thought discussed in Chapters 1–3 can largely be understood without any reference to Hegel's speculative logic, which was discussed in Chapter 4. It should be pointed out, however, that this is not the case with regard to Hegel's attempt to demonstrate the implicit rationality of the Christian religion, which for him very much depends on showing that the doctrine of the Trinity can be interpreted in terms of his speculative logic.

NOTES

INTRODUCTION

1 Hegel, G. W. F. (1977), *Phenomenology of Spirit*. A. V. Miller trans., Oxford: Oxford University Press, 24. Cited by paragraph number.
2 Hegel, G. W. F. (1991a), *The Encyclopaedia Logic*. T. F. Geraets, W. A. Suchting and H. S. Harris trans., Indianapolis: Hackett, § 14. Cited by section (§) number. The letter R indicates a remark which Hegel himself added to the section, while the letter A indicates an addition based on notes made by his students.
3 Cf. Hegel (1991a: § 13).
4 Cf. Pinkard, T. (2000), *Hegel: A Biography*. Cambridge: Cambridge University Press, 22ff.
5 Cf. Pinkard (2000: 451).
6 Hegel, G. W. F. (1984), *Hegel: The Letters*. Clark Butler and Christiane Seiler trans., Bloomington: Indiana University Press, 307.
7 Cf. Riedel, M. (1984), *Between Tradition and Revolution: The Hegelian Transformation of Political Philosophy*. Walter Wright trans., Cambridge: Cambridge University Press, 57ff.

1 HEGEL'S PHILOSOPHY OF SUBJECTIVE SPIRIT

1 Cf. Kant, I. (1929), *Critique of Pure Reason*. Norman Kemp Smith trans., Basingstoke and London: Macmillan, A 110. Cited by the first (A) and second (B) edition pagination of the Prussian Academy of Sciences edition of Kant's works.
2 Cf. Kant (1929: A 120).
3 Cf. Kant (1929: A 320/B 376).
4 Fichte, J. G. (1982), *Science of Knowledge with the First and Second Introductions*. Peter Heath and John Lachs trans., Cambridge: Cambridge University Press, 38. Cited by page number.
5 Fichte (1982: 37).
6 Cf. Fichte (1982: 35).
7 Fichte (1982: 99).

8 Kant (1929: A 113).
9 Kant (1929: B 130).
10 Cf. Kant (1929: B 133).
11 Hegel (1991a: § 24A1).
12 Hegel, G. W. F. (1971a), *Hegel's Philosophy of Mind*. William Wallace and A. V. Miller trans., Oxford: Oxford University Press, § 424A. Cited by section (§) number. The letter R indicates a remark which Hegel himself added to the section, while the letter A indicates an addition based on notes made by his students.
13 Hegel (1977: 235).
14 Hegel, G. W. F. (1991b), *Elements of the Philosophy of Right*. H. B. Nisbet trans., Cambridge: Cambridge University Press, § 25. Cited by section (§) number. The letter R indicates a remark which Hegel himself added to the section, while the letter A indicates an addition based on notes made by his students.
15 Cf. Fichte (1982: 37).
16 Cf. Fichte (1982: 246).
17 Cf. Fichte (1982: 117).
18 Cf. Fichte (1982: 12f.).
19 Cf. Hegel (1977: 26).
20 Hegel (1977: 91).
21 Cf. Hegel (1971a: § 424).
22 Cf. Hegel (1971a: § 381).
23 Cf. Hegel (1977: 159f.).
24 Cf. Hegel (1971a: § 425).
25 Hegel (1977: 177).
26 Cf. Hegel (1971a: § 436).
27 Cf. Hegel (1971a: § 432A).
28 Cf. Hegel (1971a: § 502R) and Hegel, G. W. F. (1975), *Lectures on the Philosophy of History: Introduction*. H. B. Nisbet trans., Cambridge: Cambridge University Press, 99. Cited by page number.
29 Cf. Hegel (1971a: § 431, including A).
30 Hegel (1991a: § 20R).
31 Fichte, J. G. (2000), *Foundations of Natural Right*. Michael Baur trans., Cambridge: Cambridge University Press, 18. Cited by page number.
32 Cf. Fichte (2000: 3).
33 Cf. Fichte (2000: 18ff.).
34 Fichte (2000: 31).
35 Cf. Fichte (2000: 41).
36 Fichte (2000: 44).
37 Fichte (2000: 43).
38 Fichte (2000: 42).
39 Cf. Hegel (1971a: § 435A).
40 Fichte (2000: 48).
41 Hegel (1991b: § 23).

2 OBJECTIVE SPIRIT: THE PHILOSOPHY OF RIGHT

1 Cf. Hegel (1971: § 387A).
2 Cf. Hegel (1991b: § 258R).
3 Cf. Hegel (1991a: 163A1).
4 Cf. Rousseau, J. J. (1987), *On the Social Contract*. In *The Basic Political Writings*, Donald A. Cress trans., Indianapolis: Hackett, 155.
5 Hegel (1991b: § 258R).
6 Cf. Hegel (1991a: 163A1).
7 Hegel (1991b: § 5).
8 Cf. Hegel (1991b: § 5R).
9 Hegel (1991b: § 6).
10 Hegel (1991b: § 7).
11 Cf. Hegel (1991b: § 29).
12 Cf. Hegel (1971: § 486).
13 Hegel (1991b: § 35).
14 Cf. Fichte (2000: 53).
15 Hegel (1991b: § 14).
16 Hegel (1991b: § 20).
17 Hegel (1991b: § 20A).
18 Cf. Hegel (1991b: § 36).
19 Cf. Hegel (1991b: § 37).
20 Cf. Hegel (1991b: § 29R) Kant himself defines the universal law of right as follows: 'so act externally that the free use of your choice [*Willkür*] can coexist with the freedom of everyone in accordance with a universal law'. Kant, I. (1996), *The Metaphysic of Morals*. Mary Gregor trans., Cambridge: Cambridge University Press, 231. Cited by Akademie edition page number.
21 Cf. Hegel (1991b: § 45).
22 Cf. Kant (1996: 223).
23 Cf. Kant (1996: 381).
24 Hegel (1991b: § 42).
25 Cf. Hegel (1991b: § 44).
26 Cf. Hegel (1991b: § 71R).
27 Cf. Hegel (1991b: § 94).
28 Cf. Hegel (1991b: § 104).
29 Cf. Hegel (1991b: § 118R).
30 Hegel (1991b: § 117).
31 Cf. Hegel (1991b: § 117A).
32 Hegel (1991b: § 107).
33 Hegel (1991b: § 121).
34 Hegel (1991b: § 124A).
35 Hegel (1991b: § 123).
36 Cf. Hegel (1991b: § 132R).
37 Hegel (1991b: 316A).
38 Cf. Hegel (1991b: § 135R).
39 Cf. Kant, I. (1991), *Groundwork of the Metaphysic of Morals*. H. J. Paton trans., London: Routledge, 421. Cited by Akademie edition page number.

40 Cf. Kant, I. (1993), *Critique of Practical Reason*. Lewis White Beck trans., New York: Macmillan, 27. Cited by Akademie edition page number.

41 Cf. Kant (1991: 431)

42 Cf. Kant (1996: 213f.).

43 Hegel (1991b: § 26).

44 Hegel (1991b: § 131).

45 Hegel (1991b: § 135R).

46 Cf. Hegel (1977: 430) and Hegel, G. W. F. (1999a), *On the Scientific Ways of Treating Natural Law, on its Place in Practical Philosophy, and its Relation to the Positive Sciences of Right*. In *Political Writings*. H. B. Nisbet trans., Cambridge: Cambridge University Press, 125.

47 Hegel (1991b: § 137R).

48 Hegel (1991b: § 137).

49 Hegel (1991b: § 140R).

50 Cf. Hegel (1991b: § 140R).

51 Kant (1996: 400 and 438).

52 Kant (1996: 401).

53 Cf. Kant (1996: 401).

54 Hegel (1991b: § 137).

55 Hegel (1991b: 209R).

56 Hegel (1991b: § 206).

57 Hegel (1991b: § 206).

58 Cf. Hegel (1991b: § 206R).

59 Cf. Hegel (1991b: §§ 190–191).

60 Hegel (1991b: § 183).

61 For an account of the historical significance of Hegel's separation of the concept of civil society from that of the political state see Riedel (1984: 129ff).

62 Cf. Hegel (1991b: § 147).

63 Hegel (1991b: § 268).

64 Hegel (1991b: § 147R).

65 Hegel (1991b: § 265).

66 Hegel (1991b: § 260).

67 Hegel (1975: 95).

68 Hegel (1991b: § 257).

69 Cf. Hegel (1977: 444).

70 Cf. Hegel (1991b: § 183).

71 Cf. Hegel (1999a: 132).

72 Hegel (1999a: 132) I have modified the translation.

73 Fichte (2000: 130).

74 Cf. Fichte (2000: 127).

75 This is reminiscent of Thomas Hobbes' claim that 'covenants, without the sword, are but words, and of no strength to secure a man at all'. Hobbes, T. (1957), *Leviathan*. Michael Oakeshott ed., Oxford: Basil Blackwell, 109.

76 Cf. Fichte (2000: 135).

77 Cf. Fichte (2000: 254).

78 Hegel (1999a: 132).
79 For a more detailed account of the way in which Hegel limits the political participation of many members of the modern state and his reasons for doing so see Hardimon, M. O. (1994), *Hegel's Social Philosophy: The Project of Reconciliation*. Cambridge: Cambridge University Press, 218ff.
80 Hegel (1991b: § 256).
81 Cf. Plant, R. (1983), *Hegel: An Introduction*. Oxford: Basil Blackwell, 230.
82 Hegel (1991b: § 27).
83 Hegel (1991b: § 4).
84 Cf. Hegel (1991b: § 4A).
85 Isaiah Berlin argues that the equating of what X would choose if he were something he is not, or at least not yet, with what X actually seeks and chooses, lies at the heart of all political theories of self-realization, including Hegel's, and that such confusion invites a totalitarian standpoint. Cf. Berlin. I (1958), *Two Concepts of Liberty*. Oxford: Clarendon Press, 1958, 18. When applied to Hegel, Berlin's argument completely ignores the fact that negative freedom is guaranteed by the laws and institutions of the modern state, within which it forms an essential moment, even if it is not, for Hegel, the highest form of freedom.
86 Hegel (1991b: § 30).
87 Cf. Hegel (1991b: § 248A).
88 Cf. Hegel (1991b: § 244).
89 For a more detailed account of Hegel's views on poverty and the various solutions to this problem that he discusses see Avineri, S. (1972), *Hegel's Theory of the Modern State*. Cambridge: Cambridge University Press, 147ff.; Hardimon (1994: 236ff); Wood, A. W. (1990), *Hegel's Ethical Thought*. Cambridge: Cambridge University Press, 247ff.
90 Cf. Hegel, G. W. F. (1983), *Philosophie des Rechts: Die Vorlesungen von 1819/20 in einer Nachschrift*. Dieter Henrich ed., Frankfurt am Main: Suhrkamp, 195. Cited by page number.
91 For an account of Hegel's philosophy of history which treats it more in its own right see Beiser, F. C. (1993), 'Hegel's Historicism', *The Cambridge Companion to Hegel*. F. C. Beiser ed., Cambridge: Cambridge University Press, 270ff.
92 Cf. Hegel (1975: 54).
93 Cf. Hegel (1971: § 482R).
94 Cf. Kant (1991: 428).
95 Cf. Kant (1991: 427).
96 Cf. Kant (1996: 223).
97 Hegel (1975: 90).
98 Cf. Hegel (1991b: § 2R).
99 Hegel (1991a: § 175A).
100 Cf. Ritter, J. (1982), *Hegel and the French Revolution*. Richard Dien Winfield trans., Cambridge, Massachusetts: The MIT Press, 52ff.
101 Hegel (1977: 581).

102 Hegel (1977: 589).
103 This idea is neatly captured in Marx's claim that, '*Equality* is nothing but a translation into French, i.e. into political form, of the German "*Ich = Ich*"'. Marx, K. (1992), *Early Writings*. Rodney Livingstone and Gregor Benton trans., London: Penguin, 364.
104 Cf. Hegel (1971: § 482R).
105 Cf. Hegel (1991b: § 277).
106 Cf. Hegel (1991b: § 291).
107 Cf. Hegel (1991b: §§ 305 and 306).
108 Cf. Beiser (1993: 294).
109 Cf. Marx (1992: 57ff.).

3 ART AND RELIGION

1 Cf. Hegel, G. W. F. (2003), *Vorlesungen über die Philosophie der Kunst.* Annemarie Gethmann-Siefert ed., Hamburg: Felix Meiner, 4f. Cited by page number. The edition of Hegel's lectures on aesthetics edited by one of his students, H. G. Hotho, has been shown to be highly unreliable on account of the numerous editorial inventions made by Hotho, which were motivated by his wish to give Hegel's philosophy of art the systematic form that he thought it lacked. Since the standard English translation of Hegel's lectures on this subject, Hegel, G. W. F. (1975), *Aesthetics* (2 vols). T. M. Knox trans., Oxford: Clarendon Press, is based on this edition of the lectures, I shall refer only to the student transcripts of the lectures which have so far been published, though not translated into English.
2 Cf. Hegel (2003: 4).
3 Cf. Hegel (2003: 126).
4 Cf. Hegel (2003: 134).
5 Cf. Hegel (2003: 32).
6 Cf. Hegel (2003: 33ff. and 36).
7 Cf. Hegel (2003: 160)
8 Cf. Herodotus (1981), *Herodotus I*. A. D. Godley trans., Cambridge, Massachusetts/London: Heinemann, Book II 53.
9 Cf. Hegel (1975: 51).
10 Cf. Pinkard (2000: 602).
11 Cf. Hegel, G. W. F. (2004), *Philosophie der Kunst oder Ästhetik nach Hegel. Im Sommer 1826 Mitschrift Friedrich Carl Hermann Victor von Kehler*. Annemarie Gethmann-Siefert and Bernadette Collenberg-Plotnikov eds, Munich: Wilhelm Fink, 208. Cited by page number.
12 Cf. Hegel (2003: 112).
13 Cf. Hegel (2003: 293).
14 Cf. Hegel (2003: 295).
15 Cf. Hegel (2003: 293).
16 Cf. Hegel (2003: 292).
17 Cf. Hegel (2004: 208).
18 Hegel (2003: 296).
19 Cf. Hegel (2003: 13).

20 Cf. Hegel (2003: 37).
21 Cf. Hegel (2003: 291).
22 Hegel (2003: 186).
23 Hegel (1991b: § 124R).
24 Cf. Hegel (2003: 187ff.).
25 Cf. Hegel (2003: 191ff.).
26 Cf. Hegel (2003: 194ff.).
27 Cf. Hegel (2003: 202).
28 Cf. Hegel (2003: 115).
29 Hegel (2004: 217).
30 Hegel (2003: 197).
31 Hegel, G. W. F. (1971b), *Early Theological Writings*. T. M. Knox trans., Philadelphia: University of Pennsylvania Press, 69.
32 Hegel (1971b: 85).
33 Hegel (1971b: 69).
34 Cf. Kant, I. (1998), *Religion within the Boundaries of Mere Reason*. Allen Wood and George di Giovanni eds, and trans. Cambridge: Cambridge University Press, 154. Cited by Akademie edition page number.
35 Kant (1998: 155).
36 Hegel (1971b: 140).
37 Cf. Lukács, G. (1975), *The Young Hegel*. Rodney Livingstone trans., London: Merlin Press, 18ff.
38 Cf. Hegel, G. W. F. (1985), *Lectures on the Philosophy of Religion Volume III: The Consummate Religion*. R. F. Brown, P. C. Hodgson and J. M. Stewart trans., Berkeley: University of California Press, 171. Cited by page number.
39 Hegel (1971b: 154).
40 Kierkegaard, S. (1992), *Concluding Unscientific Postscript, Volume I: Text*. Howard V. Hong and Edna H. Hong trans., Princeton, New Jersey: Princeton University Press, 33.
41 Kierkegaard therefore argues that faith requires its own indirect form of communication. Cf. Kierkegaard (1992: 72ff.).
42 Hegel, G. W. F. (1984), *Lectures on the Philosophy of Religion Volume I: Introduction and the Concept of Religion*. R. F. Brown, P. C. Hodgson and J. M. Stewart trans., Berkeley: University of California Press, 272. Cited by page number.
43 Hegel (1991a: § 62R).
44 Hegel (1991a: § 62R).
45 Cf. Jacobi, F. H. (1994), *The Main Philosophical Writings and the Novel Allwill*. George di. Giovanni trans., Montreal and Kingston: McGill–Queen's University Press, 376.
46 Hegel (1991a: § 73).
47 Hegel (1991a: § 63R).
48 Cf. Hegel (1984: 260).
49 Cf. Jacobi (1994: 563).
50 Hegel, G. W. F. (1974), *Religion and Religious Truth: Hegel's Foreword to H. Fr. W. Hinrichs' Die Religion im inneren Verhältnisse zur Wissenschaft* (1822). A. V. Miller trans., in *Beyond Epistemology: New*

Studies in the Philosophy of Hegel. Frederick G. Weiss ed., The Hague: Martinus Nijhoff, 239. Cited by page number.
51 Hegel (1974: 228) I have slightly modified the translation.
52 Hegel (1984: 106).
53 Hegel (1984: 389).
54 Cf. Hegel (1974: 231).
55 Hegel (1974: 234–235).
56 Hegel (1974: 233).
57 Hegel (1977: 537). I have slightly modified the translation.
58 Hegel (1977: 553).
59 Hegel (1977: 554).
60 Cf. Hegel (1984: 397f.).
61 Cf. Hegel (1984: 399).
62 Cf. Hegel (1984: 401).
63 Hegel (1975: 40) I have modified the translation.
64 Cf. Hegel (1991a: § 163) and Hegel, G. W. F. (1999b), *Hegel's Science of Logic.* A. V. Miller trans., New York: Humanities Press, 600ff. Cited by page number.
65 Cf. Hegel (1971a: § 567).
66 Hegel (1971a: § 568).
67 Hegel (1977: 760).
68 Hegel (1977: 762).
69 Cf. Hegel (1977: 763).
70 Cf. Strauss, D. F. (1983), *In Defense of my 'Life of Jesus' against the Hegelians.* Marilyn Chapin Massey trans., Hamden, Connecticut: Archon, 3.
71 Cf. Strauss, D. F. (1972), *The Life of Jesus Critically Examined.* George Eliot trans., Philadelphia: Fortress Press, 39ff.
72 Cf. Strauss (1972: lii).
73 Cf. Strauss (1972: 780).
74 Cf. Yerkes, J. (1983), *The Christology of Hegel.* Albany: State University of New York Press, 112.
75 Cf. Strauss (1983: 38). A selection of left-Hegelian writings can be found in Stepelevich, L. S. ed. (1983), *The Young Hegelians.* Cambridge: Cambridge University Press.
76 Cf. Kierkegaard, S. (1980), *The Sickness unto Death.* Howard V. Hong and Edna H. Hong trans., Princeton, New Jersey: Princeton University Press, 218.
77 Cf. Kierkegaard (1992: 571).
78 Kierkegaard (1992: 217).

4 PHILOSOPHY: THE METAPHYSICS OF FREEDOM

1 Hegel (1977: 37).
2 Cf. Hegel (1991a: § 20R).
3 Hegel (1999b: 25).
4 Hegel (1991a: § 60R).

5 Cf. Kant, I. (1997), *Prolegomena to Any Future Metaphysics That Will Be Able to Come Forward as Science.* Gary Hatfield trans., Cambridge: Cambridge University Press, 293. Cited by Akademie edition page number.
6 Hegel (1999b: 163). I have slightly modified the translation.
7 Cf. Hegel (1971a: § 415R).
8 Cf. Hegel (1999b: 49).
9 Hegel (1991a: § 28A).
10 Cf. Hegel (1991a: § 42R).
11 Cf. Kant (1929: A68–A69/B93–B94).
12 Cf. Fichte (1982: 21).
13 Hegel (1991a: § 28).
14 Hegel (1991a: § 24) A number of attempts have nevertheless been made to offer a non-metaphysical interpretation of Hegel's thought. For an overview of these attempts see Wartenberg, T. E., 'Hegel's idealism: The Logic of Conceptuality', in Beiser (1993: 120ff.).
15 Hegel (1977: 17).
16 Hegel (1977: 18).
17 Cf. Hegel (1999b: 580).
18 Cf. Hegel (1999b: 536).
19 Cf. Hegel (1999b: 580).
20 Cf. Hegel (1999b: 581).
21 Cf. Hegel (1999b: 536).
22 Cf. Hegel (1991a: §§ 28 and 30).
23 Spinoza, B. (1994), *The Ethics.* Part I D3. In *A Spinoza Reader.* Edwin Curley ed., Princeton: Princeton University Press.
24 Cf. Spinoza (1994: Part I P11 Dem.).
25 Cf. Spinoza (1994: Part I D4).
26 Cf. Hegel (1999b: 537).
27 Cf. Spinoza (1994: Part I P31 Dem.).
28 Cf. Spinoza (1994: Part I D5).
29 Cf. Hegel (1999b: 538).
30 Hegel (1999b: 534).
31 Hegel (1991a: § 151A).
32 Hegel (1999b: 538).
33 Cf. Hegel (1991a: § 79).
34 Hegel (1999b: 82).
35 Hegel (1999b: 82).
36 Cf. Hegel (1991a: § 87R).
37 Hegel (1991a: § 80).
38 Hegel (1999b: 90).
39 Hegel (1999b: 92).
40 Cf. Hegel (1999b: 56).
41 Cf. Hegel (1999b: 107).
42 Cf. Hegel (1991a: § 125R).
43 Hegel (1991a: § 92).
44 Hegel (1999b: 138)
45 Hegel (1999b: 50) I have slightly modified the translation.
46 Hegel (1984: 84).

47 Hegel (1984: 114).
48 Hegel (1999b: 137).
49 Hegel (1999b: 143).
50 Hegel (1991a: § 93).
51 Hegel (1999b: 149).
52 Hegel (1991a: § 94A).
53 Hegel (1991a: § 19R).
54 Cf. Hegel (1999b: 63).
55 Cf. Hegel (1991a: § 158).
56 Hegel (1991a: § 213).
57 Cf. Hegel (1991a: § 213R).
58 Cf. Hegel (1991a: § 224).

CONCLUSION

1 Hegel (1991a: § 24A2).
2 Hegel (1991b: § 31).
3 Hegel (1991b: § 272).
4 However, when Hegel comes to present his dialectical exposition of the political state, he in fact inverts the logical order of the moments of the Concept by beginning with the monarch instead of the legislature. So puzzling is this 'unintelligible' exception to the dialectical order of presenting his theories that it has been suggested that by giving prominence to the power of the monarch in this way Hegel is attempting to accommodate himself to the existing social order. Cf. Ilting, K. H. (1971), 'The Structure of Hegel's *Philosophy of Right*'. In *Hegel's Political Philosophy: Problems and Perspectives*, Z. A. Pelczynski ed., Cambridge: Cambridge University Press, 106.

FURTHER READING

Houlgate, S. (2005), *An Introduction to Hegel: Freedom, Truth and History* (2nd ed.), Oxford: Blackwell provides an introduction to all the major areas of Hegel's thought, including his philosophy of nature. It also contains a useful biographical essay. Beiser, F. C. ed. (1993), *The Cambridge Companion to Hegel*. Cambridge: Cambridge University Press contains articles on various aspects of Hegel's thought and its influence together with a bibliography. Stern, R. (2002), *Hegel and the Phenomenology of Spirit*. London: Routledge provides an overview of the work in question and an extensive bibliography together with a guide to further reading. The issue of recognition, which, as we saw in Chapter 1, has an important role to play in Hegel's theory of spirit is discussed in Williams, R. R. (1992), *Recognition: Fichte and Hegel on the Other*. Albany: State University of New York Press, 1992) and Williams, R. R. (1997) *Hegel's Ethics of Recognition*. Berkeley: University of California Press. The latter work attempts to relate the concept of recognition to Hegel's social and political thought. Two recent works that stress the importance of the concept of freedom for an understanding of Hegel's political thought are Franco, P. (1999), *Hegel's Philosophy of Freedom*. New Haven: Yale University Press and Neuhouser, F. (2000), *Foundations of Hegel's Social Theory: Actualizing Freedom*. Cambridge, Massachusetts: Harvard University Press. Jaeschke, W. (1990), *Reason in Religion: The Foundations of Hegel's Philosophy of Religion*. J. Michael Stewart and Peter C. Hodgson trans., Berkeley: University of California Press is an important work on Hegel's philosophy of religion. A good starting point for further study of Hegel's *Logic* is

Hartnack, J. (1998), *An Introduction to Hegel's Logic*. Lars Aagaard-Mogensen trans., Indianapolis: Hackett. Finally, Inwood, M. (1992), *A Hegel Dictionary*. Oxford: Blackwell is a helpful guide to Hegel's terminology.

SELECTED BIBLIOGRAPHY

PRIMARY TEXTS

Fichte, J. G. (1982), *Science of Knowledge with the First and Second Introductions*. Peter Heath and John Lachs trans., Cambridge: Cambridge University Press.

—— (2000), *Foundations of Natural Right*. Michael Baur trans., Cambridge: Cambridge University Press.

Hegel, G. W. F. (1970), *Hegel's Philosophy of Nature*. A. V. Miller trans., Oxford: Clarendon Press.

—— (1971a), *Hegel's Philosophy of Mind*. William Wallace and A. V. Miller trans., Oxford: Oxford University Press.

—— (1971b), *Early Theological Writings*. T. M. Knox trans., Philadelphia: University of Pennsylvania Press.

—— (1974), *Religion and Religious Truth: Hegel's Foreword to H. Fr. W. Hinrichs' Die Religion im inneren Verhältnisse zur Wissenschaft* (1822). A. V. Miller trans., in *Beyond Epistemology: New Studies in the Philosophy of Hegel*. Frederick G. Weiss ed., The Hague: Martinus Nijhoff.

—— (1975), *Lectures on the Philosophy of History: Introduction*. H. B. Nisbet trans., Cambridge: Cambridge University Press.

—— (1977), *Phenomenology of Spirit*. A. V. Miller trans., Oxford: Oxford University Press.

—— (1983), *Philosophie des Rechts: Die Vorlesungen von 1819/20 in einer Nachschrift*. Dieter Henrich ed., Frankfurt am Main: Suhrkamp.

—— (1984ff.), *Lectures on the Philosophy of Religion*, vols. 1–3. R. F. Brown, P. C. Hodgson and J. M. Stewart trans., Berkeley: University of California Press.

—— (1991a), *The Encyclopaedia Logic*. T. F. Geraets, W. A. Suchting and H. S. Harris trans., Indianapolis: Hackett.

—— (1991b), *Elements of the Philosophy of Right*. H. B. Nisbet trans., Cambridge: Cambridge University Press.

—— (1999a), *Political Writings*. H. B. Nisbet trans., Cambridge: Cambridge University Press.

—— (1999b), *Hegel's Science of Logic*. A. V. Miller trans., New York: Humanities Press.

—— (2003), *Vorlesungen über die Philosophie der Kunst.* Annemarie Gethmann-Siefert ed., Hamburg: Felix Meiner.

—— (2004), *Philosophie der Kunst oder Ästhetik nach Hegel. Im Sommer 1826 Mitschrift Friedrich Carl Hermann Victor von Kehler.* Annemarie Gethmann-Siefert and Bernadette Collenberg-Plotnikov eds, Munich: Wilhelm Fink.

Jacobi, F. H. (1994), *The Main Philosophical Writings and the Novel Allwill.* George di. Giovanni trans., Montreal and Kingston: McGill–Queen's University Press.

Kant, I. (1929), *Critique of Pure Reason.* Norman Kemp Smith trans., Basingstoke and London: Macmillan.

—— (1991), *Groundwork of the Metaphysic of Morals.* H. J. Paton trans., London: Routledge.

—— (1993), *Critique of Practical Reason.* Lewis White Beck trans., New York: Macmillan.

—— (1996), *The Metaphysic of Morals.* Mary Gregor trans., Cambridge: Cambridge University Press.

—— (1997), *Prolegomena to Any Future Metaphysics That Will Be Able to Come Forward as Science.* Gary Hatfield trans., Cambridge: Cambridge University Press.

—— (1998), *Religion within the Boundaries of Mere Reason.* Allen Wood and George di Giovanni eds. and trans., Cambridge: Cambridge University Press.

Kierkegaard, S. (1980), *The Sickness unto Death.* Howard V. Hong and Edna H. Hong trans., Princeton, New Jersey: Princeton University Press.

—— (1992), *Concluding Unscientific Postscript, Volume I: Text.* Howard V. Hong and Edna H. Hong trans., Princeton, New Jersey: Princeton University Press.

Rousseau, J. J. (1987), *The Basic Political Writings.* Donald A. Cress trans., Indianapolis/Cambridge: Hackett.

Spinoza, B. (1994), *A Spinoza Reader.* Edwin Curley ed., Princeton, New Jersey: Princeton University Press.

Strauss, D. F. (1972), *The Life of Jesus Critically Examined.* George Eliot trans., Philadelphia: Fortress Press.

—— (1983), *In Defense of my 'Life of Jesus' against the Hegelians.* Marilyn Chapin Massey trans., Hamden, Connecticut: Archon.

SECONDARY TEXTS

Avineri, S. (1972), *Hegel's Theory of the Modern State.* Cambridge: Cambridge University Press.

Beiser, F. C. (ed.) (1993), *The Cambridge Companion to Hegel.* Cambridge: Cambridge University Press.

Bungay, S. (1984), *Beauty and Truth: A Study of Hegel's Aesthetics.* Oxford: Oxford University Press.

Burbidge, J. (1981), *On Hegel's Logic: Fragments of a Commentary.* Atlantic Highlands, NJ: Humanities Press.

Desmond, W. (1986), *Art and the Absolute: A Study of Hegel's Aesthetics.* Albany: State University of New York Press.

Dudley, W. (2002), *Hegel, Nietzsche, and Philosophy: Thinking Freedom.* Cambridge: Cambridge University Press.

Fackenheim, E. (1967), *The Religious Dimension in Hegel's Thought.* Chicago: Chicago University Press.

Ferrarin, A. (2001), *Hegel and Aristotle.* Cambridge: Cambridge University Press.

Franco, P. (1999), *Hegel's Philosophy of Freedom.* New Haven: Yale University Press.

Gadamer, H.-G. (1976), *Hegel's Dialectic: Five Hermeneutical Studies.* P. Christopher Smith trans., New Haven: Yale University Press.

Hardimon, Michael O. (1994), *Hegel's Social Philosophy: The Project of Reconciliation.* Cambridge: Cambridge University Press.

Harris, H. S. (1972), *Hegel's Development I: Toward the Sunlight (1770–1801).* Oxford: Oxford University Press.

—— (1983), *Hegel's Development II: Night Thoughts (Jena 1801–6).* Oxford: Oxford University Press.

—— (1997), *Hegel's Ladder.* 2 vols, Indianapolis: Hackett.

Hartnack, J. (1998), *An Introduction to Hegel's Logic.* Lars Aagaard-Mogensen trans., Indianapolis: Hackett.

Houlgate, S. (1986), *Hegel, Nietzsche and the Criticism of Metaphysics.* Cambridge: Cambridge University Press.

—— (ed.) (1998), *Hegel and the Philosophy of Nature.* Albany: State University of New York Press.

—— (2005), *An Introduction to Hegel: Freedom, Truth and History* (2nd ed.). Oxford: Blackwell.

Hyppolite (1974), *Genesis and Structure of Hegel's 'Phenomenology of Spirit'.* S. Cherniak and J. Heckman trans., Evanston: Northwestern University Press.

Inwood, M. (1983), *Hegel.* London: Routledge.

—— (1992), *A Hegel Dictionary.* Oxford: Blackwell.

Jaeschke, W. (1990), *Reason in Religion: The Foundations of Hegel's Philosophy of Religion.* J. Michael Stewart and Peter C. Hodgson trans., Berkeley: University of California Press.

Knowles, D. (2002), *Hegel and the Philosophy of Right.* London: Routledge.

Kojève, A. (1969), *Introduction to the Reading of Hegel.* J. H. Nichols trans., New York: Basic Books.

Lukács, G. (1975), *The Young Hegel.* R. Livingstone trans., London: Merlin Press.

Maker, W. (ed.) (2000), *Hegel and Aesthetics.* Albany: State University of New York Press.

Marcuse, H. (1955), *Reason and Revolution: Hegel and the Rise of Social Theory* (2nd ed.). London: Routledge & Kegan Paul.

McCarney, J. (2000), *Hegel on History.* London: Routledge.

Neuhouser, F. (2000), *Foundations of Hegel's Social Theory: Actualizing Freedom.* Cambridge, Massachusetts: Harvard University Press.

O'Brien, G. (1975), *Hegel on Reason and History*. Chicago: University of Chicago Press.

Pelzcynski, Z. A. (ed.) (1971), *Hegel's Political Philosophy*. Cambridge: Cambridge University Press.

—— (ed.) (1984), *The State and Civil Society: Studies in Hegel's Political Philosophy*. Cambridge: Cambridge University Press.

Pinkard, T. (2000), *Hegel: A Biography*. Cambridge: Cambridge University Press.

Pippin, R. B. (1989), *Hegel's Idealism: The Satisfactions of Self-Consciousness*. Cambridge: Cambridge University Press.

Plant, R. (1983), *Hegel: An Introduction* (2nd ed.). Oxford: Basil Blackwell.

Riedel, M. (1984), *Between Tradition and Revolution: The Hegelian Transformation of Political Philosophy*. Walter Wright trans., Cambridge: Cambridge University Press.

Ritter, J. (1982), *Hegel and the French Revolution*. R. D. Winfield trans., Cambridge, Mass.: MIT Press.

Rosen, S. (1974), *G. W. F. Hegel: An Introduction to the Science of Wisdom*. New Haven: Yale University Press.

Solomon, R. (1983), *In the Spirit of Hegel: A Study of G. W. F. Hegel's 'Phenomenology of Spirit'*. Cambridge: Cambridge University Press.

Stern, R. (1990), *Hegel, Kant and the Structure of the Object*. London: Routledge.

—— (2002), *Hegel and the Phenomenology of Spirit*. London: Routledge.

Stewart, J. (ed.) (1998), *The 'Phenomenology of Spirit' Reader: Critical and Interpretative Essays*. Albany: State University of New York Press.

—— (2000), *The Unity of Hegel's 'Phenomenology of Spirit'*. Evanston: Northwestern University Press.

—— (2003), *Kierkegaard's Relations to Hegel Reconsidered*. Cambridge: Cambridge University Press.

Stone, A. (2005), *Petrified Intelligence: Nature in Hegel's Philosophy*. Albany: State University of New York Press.

Taylor, C. (1975), *Hegel*. Cambridge: Cambridge University Press.

—— (1979), *Hegel and Modern Society*. Cambridge: Cambridge University Press.

Westphal, K. (2003), *Hegel's Epistemology: A Philosophical Introduction to the Phenomenology of Spirit*. Indianapolis: Hackett.

Westphal, M. (1998), *History and Truth in Hegel's 'Phenomenology'* (3rd ed.). Bloomington: Indiana University Press.

Williams, R. R. (1992), *Recognition: Fichte and Hegel on the Other*. Albany: State University of New York Press.

—— (1997) *Hegel's Ethics of Recognition*. Berkeley: University of California Press.

Wood, A. W. (1990), *Hegel's Ethical Thought*. Cambridge: Cambridge University Press.

Yerkes, J. (1983), *The Christology of Hegel*. Albany: State University of New York Press.

INDEX